E. C Sim

Our Travels round the World 1892-94

E. C Sim

Our Travels round the World 1892-94

ISBN/EAN: 9783744716871

Printed in Europe, USA, Canada, Australia, Japan

Cover: Foto ©Andreas Hilbeck / pixelio.de

More available books at **www.hansebooks.com**

OUR TRAVELS

ROUND THE WORLD.

1892-94.

BY

MAJOR-GENERAL E. C. SIM.

LONDON:
ALEXANDER AND SHEPHEARD,
21, FURNIVAL ST., HOLBORN.

1897.

IN revising the numbers of "Our Travels Round the World," reprinted from *The Royal Engineers' Journal* for circulation among my friends, I wish to express the great assistance received from my wife and daughter in the copious notes kept by them, without which I could not have written anything.

I trust that my next paper will be about India, "the brightest jewel of the British Crown," which I think every Englishman ought to visit, at all events once in his life.

E. C. SIM,

July, 1896. *Major-General.*

CONTENTS.

		PAGE
PART I.	OUTWARD BOUND	7
PART II.	WESTERN AUSTRALIA	19
PART III.	SINGAPORE AND SIAM	31
PART IV.	CHINA	41
PART V.	JAPAN	62
PART VI.	VOYAGING SOUTH	74
PART VII.	SOUTH SEA ISLANDS	85
PART VIII.	AUSTRALASIA	96
PART IX.	NEW ZEALAND	118
PART X.	HOMEWARD BOUND	129

OUR TRAVELS ROUND THE WORLD.

I.

In October, 1892, having been strongly advised to take an ocean voyage for the benefit of my health, and to avoid the cold and fogs of a winter in England, we decided to start for Western Australia, where I had some business connected with a Land Grant Railway; and also I wished to see many old friends with whom I had kept up a correspondence, &c., for thirty years, as I had been stationed at the old Swan River Convict Settlement in Western Australia for several years—1858 to 1862.

When you make up your mind to start for a place on the other side of the world your first impression—or at least mine—is to take as many clothes as you can; we meant to have stayed six or eight months, and, therefore, wanted "things," but it is a great mistake; the trouble of moving baggage after you leave ocean steamers and in land or railway transit is very great, and often very expensive, as in

Australia, America, and other places. I therefore propose to put down the necessary articles you should take under the head of :—"C," coin, in gold or notes; clothes, few as possible; camphor; charts, terrestrial and celestial; cinchona (quinine), a little; Cook's guides; cigarettes and cigars; chairs, comfortable; collars, many; chiffons, ladies'; cognac, good; chocolates, for the ladies; condensed soup; collections of books and magazines; chlorodyne; carbolic soap; cards, playing and visiting; cribbage board; corkscrew, very necessary; chronometer, barometer and thermometer; code telegram, unicode published by Cassell & Co., most useful, cost about 2s. 6d. While I am on this subject, I should say always have £100 in hand, which for a party of three is sufficient in case of accidents, as our total average expenditure in eighteen months was about £120 a month.

Having made up our minds what we should take, we decided to embark in a fairly large 3,500-ton steamer—the ss. *Nairnshire*, bound for Fremantle, Western Australia, with a general cargo, but whose principal business in life was to bring home frozen meat—I believe something like 50,000 carcases of sheep—and had, therefore, excellent machinery. She was engined and, I believe, built by my friends Hawthorn, Leslie & Co., of Newcastle, whose chairman, Sir B. C. Browne, had been two or three times Mayor of Newcastle-on-Tyne, and is also connected with W.A. Railways. His brother, Captain C. O. Browne, late R.A., was a contemporary of mine, and is a lecturer and authority on iron and steel, probably known to many of our officers. The freezing or cold storage engines of these steamers are very ingenious, have to be kept in first-rate order, if the cargo is to be delivered sound in London, and they can produce perfect snow in the tropics, the passengers on the homeward voyage sometimes indulging in snow-balling. We, however, were never even allowed to have any ice on the outward route.

On a raw, foggy, gloomy afternoon we left the S.W. India Docks on the top of the tide, I suppose, for if we had not left then we were told we could not have got out for ten days or a fortnight; we had a large general cargo, and a great deal of railway iron, and a steam pinnace as a deck "passenger," going out for the Government of Western Australia, which made us "roll" a great deal.

We had about thirty saloon passengers, some of them intending to stick to the ship all round the world. I believe they paid about £70, which for at least four months' voyaging was not much, being under 12s. a day, a very fair table being kept, and good claret and whiskey to be purchased at reasonable rates; there was also capital beer.

We paid for ourselves, a party of three, with an excellent cabin (off the saloon) and a good ladies' cabin for the young ladies, 100 guineas, which for fifty days was very moderate; but I happened to know the charterers.

We dropped down the river to Gravesend on 25th October (being towed so far), and anchored for the night; many friends came to see us off in London, but we made such a flying start from the docks, on account of the tide serving earlier than was expected, that many were unable to get on board, and we waved our farewells from the quarter deck, for our good ship was flush-decked, and had a walk round of nearly one-tenth of a mile. This is a very important matter on an ocean voyage, as you must take some sort of exercise; ten times round equals a mile is easy to remember. I believe our steamer was exactly 365 feet long, which was also easy to bear in mind.

She was what is called generally a ten-knot steamer, could do twelve at a pinch, and I should think averaged nine knots, but I will tell you more of this later on ; the distance was, say, 10,000 miles, fifty days equal 200 knots a day. We were actually steaming forty-seven days, thirty-seven days of which we never stopped, except occasionally for an hour to screw up something, or ease the engines, &c. After leaving Gravesend and dropping down the river, we had rather rough and boisterous weather; our captain's wife, who had accompanied us so far, went off in a Deal boat under sail, bobbing up and down like a cork, and we watched her proceedings with great interest, for we thought the boat would capsize; but Deal boats are not built that way, and she reached Deal beach in safety.

We could not land our pilot at Dover, as it was blowing too hard; the Downs and his responsibility ended here, but we had to carry him on to Portland, and after steaming round Weymouth Bay several times, for it was very thick and overcast, we managed to get a Channel tug to take him off by a series of bribes, otherwise he would have been carried on to Las Palmas, in the Canary Islands.

It is curious that Portland should also be the residence of certain canary-clothed gentry, about whom I will discourse later on. It is a grand promontory as seen from the sea. Between Portland and Ushant (the great light you always notice before you reach the Bay of Biscay) the weather was "fresh," which means we pitched and rolled about cheerfully, but after Ushant, and when we were expecting worse weather, the wind moderated, and we slipped down the coast of Portugal and Spain very pleasantly, until after ten days' "yachting" we arrived at Las Palmas in Grand Canary, a very beautiful port which I will describe later on.

I rather wish to digress at this stage of our tale, because I had been thirty-five years before almost over the same ground in a convict ship with a detachment of Sappers as a guard going out to Western Australia to relieve a portion of 20th Company, R.E., who had been sent home with then Lieutenants Du Cane and Crossman, R.E., to take part in the Crimean War, should their services have been required, in 1855-6, which was not the case, as the war ended. Sir Edmund Henderson, then a 1st Captain, had accompanied them home.

We left the old R.E.E., Chatham, on 1st September, 1857, on a lovely summer or autumn morning, being marched out by the present Sir Charles Nugent, then our adjutant, with the new R.E. Band then being formed, and we embarked at Deptford Dockyard, where the good or bad convict ship *Nile* was being fitted for her voyage.

We had a Captain, R.E., now dead, I am sorry to say, Thorold, my brother subaltern, myself, and about thirty men, women, and children, and if I might allude to our passengers, we had our captain's wife, two charming little children, and two maid-servants, who took up the accommodation meant for us subalterns. Fancy this on a convict ship, on which there is always a chance of an outbreak, and yet habitually officers' and pensioners' wives with their families were sent out in this way. The pensioners usually formed the guard on board ship, and garrisoned Fremantle, Western Australia, afterwards—where about 200 men were always enrolled for duty, to guard magazines, prisons, convicts, &c. We had on board the *Nile* the Bishop Designate of Perth, W.A., his chaplain, and a young friend, beside the Surgeon, R.N., Superintendent, who flew a transport pennant and commanded the whole. Our ship captain, who eventually joined us at Plymouth, and had recently lost a ship off Ceylon, was new to the employment, and not very cheerful. The only port we touched at on the voyage out was Bahia in Brazil, a lovely spot, where we fitted a new main topmast and stayed a week. This voyage, about which I hope to write an account at some future time, with our cargo of 300 convicts and rather a varied assortment of passengers, occupied about 100 days under sail after leaving Plymouth on 20th September, 1857, reaching Fremantle on New Year's Day, 1858, and it took us 168 days to return from Western Australia in 1862, when I came home in command of 20th Company, about thirty men, ninety women and children, with Thorold and his family, and a Staff-Surgeon, R.N., in medical charge.

I only mention these former voyages to show what a fearful waste of time there was in the " good old days " in moving troops about the world. I used to say that the only time I ever saved any money in the service was on my return with the 20th Company, R.E., from Western Australia, when I had six months' pay due to me in England. On that occasion we put into Simon's Bay, Cape Colony, to " refit," for a week or ten days ; and afterwards called at St. Helena for water.

To return to Palmas in Grand Canary, it seemed to us a beautiful harbour, with many ships calling for coal, both going from and returning to England. We were, however, placed in quarantine, as once upon a time an old lady had nearly died from cholera at Gravesend, which was our last port of departure.

So the local authorities at Palmas would not allow us to land or communicate with the shore, except through a dirty little police-boat with a tattered constable in it, who made fast to a stone anchor, and bobbed up and down serenely for about two days, while we were coaling and taking in fruit, which is most abundant here; we bought oranges and bananas enough to last us nearly a month, and very cheap.

The views of the island from the roadstead are most picturesque; through a gap you could see the peak of Teneriffe, sixty miles away, quite distinctly; and the luxurious vegetation round an excellent hotel about two miles distant, and much used in winter by delicate visitors, made us long to go ashore.

I suggested to our skipper that £5 judiciously bestowed would probably overcome the scruples of the Custom House officers, because this would be in Spanish money I don't know how many pesetas; but the captain, being a canny Scot, did not see the object of parting with his English coin, and perhaps being fined into the bargain, so we coaled and dirtied our ship and clothes; and in addition, took more than 100 tons forward on deck, to help our good old ship to reach her coaling port—Newcastle, in N.S. Wales—fourteen days beyond Fremantle. Her consumption, with triple expansion engines, &c., was only about twenty tons a day, and she could take 1,200 tons easily.

We left Palmas on the 5th November in fine weather, and "jogged" along at our usual ten knots down the coast of Africa, occasionally sighting high land and lighthouses, with a few steamers of opposition lines trading to the Cape. It was getting pretty hot, too, as there was little or no wind ; and we crossed the line on 12th November, just a week after leaving Palmas. My notes say lat. 00·00, long. 7°, 21' W., November 12th, 1892 ; distance run 238 miles last twenty-four hours. We had no "larks" on crossing the line, as our captain was a dour old Scot, and cared not for these "antics." Our lives were consequently very placid ; we read, played cribbage, Khanhoo—a most excellent Chinese game—of which more later on, and whist. We had singing parties in the saloon ; some of the ladies had mandolines and guitars, but their *répertoire* was limited, and we got a little tired of "Funiculi-Funicula" on piano and mandolines with chorus.

I kept the chart and logged the run daily; we had quoits, cricket, and "sweeps" on the run. Our chairs were very comfortable, and if it had not been for a frisky family of children who disturbed our slumbers, we should probably have slept more.

On 24th November we sighted Cape Town a long way off, and there was a great deal of fog about. I noted in my diary "syren" blowing ; but as we had no cargo or orders for the Cape, we discontented ourselves with making the Cape of Good Hope lighthouse and signal station high upon the mountain—the mist lifting like a cap just as we had shifted our course to the southward ; for steamers expect to be reported from this place, which is one of the magnificent Lloyd's stations, now nearly all over the civilised world.

After this our voyage became very uneventful ; it was generally cooler ; we hardly sighted a ship, and only occasionally saw a whale.

We went south to about 42°, when, as the westerly winds were not favourable, we altered our course more to the north, and so escaped the cold.

About four or five days off the coast of Western Australia (which we sighted early on 13th December, about 2 a.m., in the shape of Rottnest Lighthouse, lat. 32° S.) we found ourselves in a sea fog, which lasted, as far as I can recollect, about two days, and although there was nothing visible near us, except albatrosses and whales, we sounded our "syren" or foghorn regularly at intervals of about five minutes, a very wearying and weird sound on the ocean.

Having come to the end of this comparatively long voyage we were received most hospitably by the Governor, Sir William F. C. Robinson, G.C.M.G., by the Premier, Sir John Forrest and Lady Forrest, by the Colonial Surgeon, Dr. Waylen, a very old friend of mine, who came to Fremantle to meet us, and with whom and his kind wife we stayed for nearly a month in the genial society of Perth, about which I propose to tell you in the next number. The weather—their midsummer—was very hot.

During our voyage we had splendid opportunities of observing the heavens at night, the stars being most brilliant in the southern hemisphere. The moon was, if anything, too bright.

I borrowed a work on "Astronomy" from one of the officers, but one always ought to take these books, as it is a most interesting subject to study. Orion, the Pleiades, Southern Cross, Leo, Canopus, and last, but not least, "Canis," the dogstars, large and small, were always visible. We had a joke that whenever you asked the skipper the name of a particular star, he said, "It's just Carnis." He was sometimes right, but was naturally not always so, and we were under the impression he could not see, and veiled his want of information under a general axiom. However, he was a good navigator and strict disciplinarian, although he occasionally chewed tobacco, and tried to get the best of us at four-handed cribbage, at which he was an adept. He was continually painting his ship, and caulking and scraping decks, which, in the early morning, when you want to sleep, between four and seven a.m., is rather distressing. I think our decks did leak into the cabins, because he furled our "awning" soon after we left the Cape, as he said it stopped our way, and we consequently had heat and glare quite unnecessary ; but it opened the seams of his decks, and so did him. The albatrosses and sea birds were very fine, and as they circled and swooped down upon the steamer and then quickly followed in its wake you fancied you could almost touch them. What rest they got is hard to say, for we distinctly recognised the same birds for hundreds of miles. I suppose they slept on the wing or on the water. One drawback we had was shifting coal from the deck forward into the bunkers. This took place some time after we left Palmas, but it caused us all to be sooty and out of temper, as you cannot keep out coal dust anywhere. The chief engineer, whom we called "Old King Coal," seemed to delight in the occupation, and came among us like a festive sweep. The smoking cabin on deck was the great object of attraction, even for some of the ladies ; it certainly was sheltered, but as it would not contain everyone on board, I usually gave it a wide berth, and smoked and slept in my grand old chair, which, having been purchased months before in Madeira, had already voyaged to the West Indies and America and back. We had a very fair cook, whom I used to consult about the change in our diet table, and we really had very little to complain of in our seven weeks' "menus." We carried some twenty second-class passengers, who were very amusing, as they nearly all had such peculiar ideas about Australia and its inhabitants. One old lady, aged I should say nearly eighty, was going out to join her family, whom she had not seen for forty years; she was only kept alive by great care and attention. Then the young ladies, who had been rather shabby on board, when we disembarked, landed in all their war-paint and finery, quite things of beauty, &c.

An old miner, who was going out to Melbourne, told me he was sure there was a lot of gold near Hampton Plains, in Western Australia, about which I had been consulted years before; he meant to have a look at it; and he was right, for a short time afterwards the Coolgardie goldfield was discovered close to it. I hope he made his pile; I did not believe in it at the time, but when I said good-bye to him in Perth a month later he tried to persuade me to go up there—300 miles in the bush—to prospect and take up blocks. These miners can almost smell gold.

The only real grievance we had was that the skipper would not read Divine service on Sundays, because he was a Presbyterian. A Church of England clergyman (a passenger) said he was too ill, and had no voice; he was going round the world for his health. One old gentleman passenger, with serious views, declined the honour of officiating, and I was not asked; so we had no service on Sundays at all, which I take to be a great misfortune. Most of the seamen were foreigners—Dutchmen, Danes, Germans, Swedes, Russians—and the boatswain had the greatest difficulty in making them understand anything, as they could not speak English. No grog was allowed, lime juice and oatmeal water only being served out daily. The most respectable Englishman in the crew had been a Governor's coachman in South Australia, and he was making his way out again at 1s. a month.

However, we all arrived safe and sound, after our seven weeks' journey, and, thanks to an all-wise Providence, I was in much better health than when we started, and my wife and daughter thoroughly enjoyed the long ocean voyage to Australia.

II.

On our arrival at Fremantle, 13th December, 1892, we found the weather very hot; it was approaching their midsummer, and the white sand and glare near the port and Swan River were very trying. Naturally the place was very much improved since I left it in April, 1862, but, of course, the features of the country and outline of the town were the same, although there was now a railway, bridges, and a breakwater being constructed to improve the harbour accommodation, and enable large steamers to discharge their cargoes alongside of the pier with safety at all times of the year. In former days there was only an open roadstead protected at a considerable distance (nearly ten miles) by the Rottnest and Garden Islands. When it came on to blow from the north and west, ships had to shift their anchorage under Garden Island for protection, causing great delay and expense. The proprietors of the cargo boats which were used for discharging made handsome profits, and enabled them to set up as merchants and legislators from being simple whalers and boatmen, but they had to work hard in all weathers. A very good railway pier has been built, which connects with the line of railway to Perth, Guildford, and the interior.

The public buildings, church, stores, &c., have been well

constructed, and I walked one day round to the old sapper and pensioner barracks ; to the large convict prison, and Sir Edmund Henderson's pretty house (now an infirmary), and thought they looked small by comparison with the new buildings ; but in the former days when we lived in them we thought them palatial, particularly the official houses.

The railway to Perth crosses the Swan River by a fine bridge below the road bridge, built perhaps twenty-five years before ; in my time there was only a ferry worked by convicts, a punt on a hawser, at which I had been nearly drowned while the convicts were repairing it after a storm in 1861. The railway line winds through North Fremantle —formerly a pensioner village—to Cottesloe, so called after the peer of that name, whose ancestor had been, I think, the Secretary for the Colonies when Western Australia was founded in 1829.

The gum trees, banksias, black boys or xanthorea, cabbage palms, &c., looked very much as I remembered them thirty-five years before, when we used to ride along a bush track by Freshwater Bay on the Swan River to Perth from Fremantle ; but houses have been built on all available sites, gardens have been made, vines planted, and much land fenced in for all sorts of purposes, and I understand that the value of the land is increasing every day in these towns and suburban lots, as the necessities of Perth require any amount of vegetables, fruit, &c., to be cultivated, often by Chinamen. The railway skirts round the north end of Mount Eliza, the pretty wooded hill overlooking the Capital, until you reach Perth— beautifully situated on the Swan River—twelve miles from Fremantle, by road and rail, and fifteen miles by the river, which winds very much. The front of the city slopes towards the river, screened by gardens, plantations, and woods. The river widens very much here, and is called Melville Water, and looks more like a lake with many houses on the banks, and when we saw it often bathed in bright moonlight, was most romantic in appearance.

The Government House, almost in the centre of the city, is a castellated red brick mansion, designed originally by Sir Edmund Henderson in 1859 (he was then Captain, R.E., and Comptroller-General of Convicts), with turrets very much like the R.M.A. at Woolwich. We were employed under Sir Edmund carrying out all the works, roads and bridges of the Colony, and I was in charge at Perth. We had an excellent Clerk of Works, Mr. James Manning, only lately dead at a good old age, being nearly 80, but whom I saw in 1893 alive and well after service under the Crown and Colony of, I should say, forty years ; he lived and died at Fremantle.

The Colonial Clerk of Works, Mr. Jewell, who was my principal assistant and instructor in 1858-61 at Perth, went away, I think, to other Colonies. At all events I did not see him in 1893. He was much respected.

The Government House was constructed by means of convict labour with sapper mechanics and instructors under Sergeant Nelson, R.E. (an admirable man), who had also assisted Captain (now General) H. Wray, R.E., C.M.G., to erect the lighthouse at Breaksea Island, off the Southern Port of Albany, King George's Sound, in 1856-7.

The Government House has been much improved by the addition of a large ball-room, &c., which it badly wanted. I believe the total cost up to 1862, when we left, and it was nearly finished, was about £4,000 including stores from England. I dare say the extras, with the ball-room, nearly doubled the expense, but if it cost only £8,000 it was a cheap house. I believe it is very comfortable, not too much room, with a beautiful view and a lovely garden.

The new public offices and post office on the site of the old soldiers' barracks are most creditable to the place ; what they cost I do not know, but something considerable. They are built of stone with brick interior work. Behind them is the town hall, a very fine structure, built, I believe, in the days of Governor Hampton, 1862-7, partly by convict labour.

The Cathedral stands in the centre of St. George's Square hard by, on the site of the old church or cathedral, I remember, built about 1835, which nearly subsided. The present red brick edifice is really very handsome, and suitable for the climate.

The house in which we stayed with our friends, Dr. and Mrs. Waylen, looked over the river, with a lovely garden all round. They had a plentiful supply of water lately obtained by this city from the Darling Range, twenty miles off ; in fact everyone was revelling in the water supply for their gardens, and as evening approached the "fair maids of Perth" with flexible hoses all appeared to water their flowers and lawns at the same time, which gave the main thoroughfares quite a festive appearance.

We attended a most excellent performance of "The Mountebanks" by the Perth Amateur Operatic Society, on the 16th December, 1892. One of the principal parts was taken by Captain Stuart, A.D.C., a son of our old friend General W. J. Stuart, R.E., and a capital actor ; in fact, everything he undertook he did well. Cricket and games of all sorts came quite handy to him, and when he left for

India to join Sir George White's staff, in January, 1893, he was "teapotted" by the club and much regretted by all his numerous friends. He was a first-rate A.D.C.

A week after we arrived in Perth the Christmas festivities seemed to begin. Some people filled their houses with friends from the country, others went off to spend their Christmas with relatives in the country; everyone made arrangements to enjoy themselves with the thermometer 85° to 90°. Race meetings were organised, boating and fishing parties got up, and all business and legislation ceased for nearly a fortnight. It was as much as housekeepers could do to get food for themselves and visitors, the principal shops being shut for the holidays.

We managed, however, to do pretty well; we had an excellent dinner party at Government House, a dance also, with first-rate music, the Governor being himself a most accomplished musician. He has since written an opera, which was performed last year in Melbourne, and we had one of the best singers in the Colony in the person of the Chief Justice.

Sir James Lee-Steere, the Speaker of the Legislative Assembly, an old friend of mine, with his family, entertained us most royally, and Sir George Shenton, the new President of the Council, did the same. I had known both the legislators in the days when we were governed by dear old Sir Arthur Kennedy, then a Captain lately retired from 68th Regiment, a most hospitable and genial Irish gentleman and a thorough sportsman, who governed many Colonies afterwards, and died on his way home from Queensland a few years ago, almost "in harness," and deeply regretted. I have every reason to remember the hospitality of his family when I was a gay young subaltern.

I went one day, a very hot one, to assist in opening the new railway to Pinjarra—forty miles—down south, which eventually was extended to Bunbury and the Vasse, about 100 miles from Perth; there was only one rather difficult place at a bridge over the Murray River, near Pinjarra, where we lunched in a most comfortable manner, had speeches from the Premier and others, and got back to Perth about 10 p.m. after a twelve hours' very agreeable outing. There are several large steam sawing timber stations on this railway.

I had ridden all over this country thirty-three years before when a subaltern, looking after roads and bridges, and it was very interesting to me to see and hear the iron horse snorting in the "bush" where formerly we saw nothing but parrots and kangaroos. I think the enterprise of Western Australia with regard to railways has been something marvellous of late years. With a population in 1892 of about 50,000, there was one railway to Albany *viâ* York and Beverley, nearly 300 miles; another railway to Pinjarra and Bunbury, say 100 miles; a line called the Midland, in which we were interested, from Guildford, ten miles north-east of Perth, to Geraldton, in the north, nearly 300 miles, partially made; and several lines to mining centres, since constructed, which easily made up another 200 miles. Total 900 miles. This is all done within the last ten years, and if they go on at the present rate you will be able to get anywhere by railway in the year 1900.

There are telegraph lines and stations all over the country, say from north to south about 2,500 miles, with a connection with South Australian lines by Eucla and a duplicate line to Singapore *viâ* Bangi-Wangi, in Batavian or Dutch East Indian Islands, from Broome, in the Kimberley district of Western Australia, the head-quarters of the pearling industry, and where Messrs. Streeter have a large depôt and fleet of pearl-fishing boats.

Telegraphing is also a cheap luxury, and people use it, I think, more in proportion than in England; but it was rather a new toy to them. You get English and foreign colonial news a few hours old every day at the club, where formerly we were lucky to get "mail" news once a month—six weeks old.

The new club, called after Governor Sir F. Weld (who did much for the colony ten years before), was opened by the Governor when we were there—a champagne tea and capital speeches—immediately after a wedding. It is beautifully situated, overlooking the river, and most comfortable, having several bedrooms for members.

We attended the races in New Year's week for two days, both very hot. I think there were three days' racing altogether. You could get to the course, five miles off, by road, river, or rail. I went by the latter and returned by the former; the river, being near the bottom of the course, was handy, but difficult to navigate.

We had excellent lunches—any amount of champagne—and I saw many old friends, most of whom had a turn at the large "totalizator"—public betting not being allowed. The attendance was very large. Some of the home-bred horses were very good, and the public generally were determined to amuse themselves. The hot weather made them very thirsty, but with the exception of the driving on return

to Perth by the road over the Long Swan Bridge and
Causeway being rather wild, there was little or nothing to
complain of. We thoroughly enjoyed our New Year
festivities.

We went for a day's outing up to Gin-Gin and the Moore
River by the Midland Railway, in which I was interested,
about eighty miles north from Perth, returning in the
afternoon by the same well-laid line, after an excellent lunch
off wood-pigeons, &c., at Gin-Gin. I crossed the temporary
wooden bridge over the Moore River on the engine, and as
the line on each side was very light, and the gradients steep,
I was very glad to get back again without accident. The
line had been made about eighty miles from Geraldton in
the southerly direction to reach the line from the Moore
River, so that altogether about 160 miles of railway out
of 300 had been completed.

We made one more excursion into the country to see my
old friends Mr. and Mrs. Sam. Phillips, of Culham, beyond
Toodjay, about sixty miles by rail east from Perth, on a
branch of the Government Railway to Northam, York, and
Beverley. We were met at the nearest railway station,
Newcastle, by an old friend of mine who was the station-
master, and drove over ten miles of pretty country to
Culham, where we spent two happy days with my friends
the Phillipses, in a house which I had seen built in 1858, and
where we said farewell to them in 1893. He was a capital
whip and his wife a charming lady and hostess.

The time had now come when we had to make up our
minds about our future route; my son, who was with an
architect in England, wired that he could not join us in
Western Australia, so we decided to take passages in a very

nice new steamer of Messrs. Holt & Co., a large Liverpool firm well known in this part of the world and China, to Singapore. Fortunately, the two Messrs. Gwyn, gentlemen connected with the firm of Bethell & Co., much interested in W.A. steamers, were going as far as Geraldton also, and they enabled us to travel at most reasonable rates. I think we only paid sixty guineas for three passages, which voyage lasted nearly twenty days, or £1 1s. a day each person.

We left Perth on the afternoon of the 9th January in the Government steam launch on the river Swan for Fremantle with a few of our most intimate friends. The Premier and his talented wife, Lady Forrest, had given us a most agreeable dinner-party on 7th inst. to meet the Governor and the *élite* of Perth, and we said good-bye on the 8th—Sunday—to some of our kind and hospitable friends with whom we had spent a most agreeable month.

I gave a small dinner party at the principal hotel at Fremantle on the evening of 9th January to my dear old friends Dr. and Mrs. Waylen, just before we embarked on board the s.s. *Saladin* for the north and Singapore; and we all drank each other's health until the time came for us to see them off at the railway station, while we went to our second ocean home to prepare for the voyage to Singapore.

It was a lovely day when we left Fremantle on 10th January, 1893, twenty-eight days after we had arrived there from England.

Our Captain Pitts was a thorough English sailor and gentleman, who understood the inhabitants and the coast; for we had rather a festive party on board after the races and New Year's festivities, but they were kept in admirable order.

We had a capital steward and stewardess, both English, with a wonderful talking parrot, a capital cook, excellent accommodation, and very pretty saloon, with good smoking room, and a music gallery with a piano for the ladies; all these were in the forward part of the steamer, which is most desirable in the tropics.

The *Saladin* was called a miniature P. and O. steamer, of about 1,200 tons, because she had been built expressly for this traffic between Western Australia and Singapore, where it is nearly always hot, and people disembarking at Singapore from England like to have a superior steamer to complete the voyage to Fremantle.

You can reach Western Australia in forty days easily by this route; much cheaper than if you go out by P. & O. or Orient lines, and also avoiding a long 300 miles' railway journey from Albany, K.G. Sound, to Perth and Fremantle.

We called at Geraldton, in Champion Bay, about 300 miles north of Fremantle, on 11th January, staying there twenty-four hours, and enabling us to see many of our old friends on hospitable thoughts intent; we then shaped our course for Shark's Bay and Peron Peninsula, where we had cargo to discharge and take in, also passengers and horses.

I had been at Geraldton before, in 1858, with our then Bishop (with whom I had come out from England), a most earnest Missionary Churchman, thorough sportsman, and bushman also. I had ridden all over this country with him, helping him to conduct the services and baptize the children, who only saw a parson about once a year, even if then. We parted at the Moore River, riding south in October, 1858—

he going to Perth and I to Gin-Gin and Toodjay to inspect roads.

After leaving Shark's Bay, a most sandy, uninviting looking place, we called at Carnarvon, on the Gascoyne River, at Onslow, on the Ashburton River, at Cossack, in Nickol Bay, near Roeburne and the Pilbarra Goldfields, where we stayed more than a day to inspect a new steam launch, &c. We then went on to Broome, in Roebuck Bay, which, as I said before, is the headquarters of the pearling industry, as far as Messrs. Streeter are concerned, and the point of departure of the ocean telegraph to Batavia and Singapore by the Island of Bali and Bangi-Wangi.

At Broome, where there is a tremendous rise and fall in the tide, and where we cannoned off the receiving hulk and damaged our bulwarks, we said farewell to Western Australia on the 20th January, and I sent telegrams to my friends in Perth and in England to announce our whereabouts.

We had a great deal of heavy rain about here, and once crossed a magnetic shoal, which made all the needle compasses go round and round. Unfortunately, I was not on deck at the time, but my ladies saw it.

After about two days from Broome you get into the lovely Batavian or Javanese Archipelago, very beautiful islands, and near the Straits of Lombok, which we traversed, the Dutch have lately been fighting the Sultan and native Rajahs.

On 23rd we called at the island of Bali for telegrams and orders; a most picturesque little port, with people of all sorts and colours.

We had no orders for Sourabaya or Batavia, so we went on gaily through the Straits, and passed beautiful islands all well lighted, for the Dutch Government seem very particular about their lighthouses, and on 28th January, 1893, we arrived at Singapore and made fast to the old Tanjong-Pagar wharf, a place which I had not seen since I returned from China in 1871—twenty-two years before ; of this more anon.

In this twenty days' voyage you have practically only two or three days' ocean work ; it is all lovely warm yachting, and most interesting, seeing new islands every day.

I am afraid that I have been more diffuse than I intended about our visit to Western Australia, but it shall not occur again. Having been my first station abroad as a subaltern, I naturally take a great interest in it now ; in fact, I never heard of anyone who had been there not wishing to go back again, and I do hope and trust that with these comparatively modern gold discoveries Western Australia has a great future. Sir Roderick Murchison, I believe, fifty years ago always said gold would be found there, and they called the River Murchison after him, and it is near that river and at Pilbarra and Kimberley in the north, and Yilgarn and Coolgardie east of Perth, that the principal goldfields are located.

Much population has been attracted to the hitherto barren wastes of Western Australia by these gold discoveries, and I trust that permanent good will be done to the old Swan River settlement by this recent development.

III.

On arrival at Singapore, 28th January, 1893, we found that the Governor, Sir Cecil Clementi-Smith, G.C.M.G., was away at Malacca, and was not expected back for some days. Sir Charles Warren, however, was most kind and hospitable, and we stayed two days with him at his pretty house on the top of a hill in the direction of Tanglin—where are also the barracks and the beautiful public gardens—about four miles from the city.

We also stayed for two or three days at the Hôtel de l'Europe, near the cricket ground, esplanade, and Cathedral, and were most comfortable. The principal part of the hotel is in dtaeched pavilions, with large airy rooms, and a central pavilion where visitors dine ; the pavilion at the entrance being used for billiards, reading-room, &c., with capital wide verandahs ; punkahs nearly everywhere, and the people seem to lead a very luxurious life.

Enormous improvements have been made since I passed through in 1868 on my way to China, and in 1871 when I returned, for Singapore has been very prosperous as a Crown Colony. New streets have been laid out ; a large hill removed to improve the road to Tanjong-Pagar, where all the large P. & O. and other steamers land their cargo alongside wharves in the narrow strait which bounds Singapore on the western side. Singapore itself being an island, called Prince-of-Wales, and having the open sea nearly all round, you get a breeze and comparatively cool nights, when at other places near the Equator (Singapore being only 2° N.) you would have perpetual heat. We were there, certainly, in the winter, and had cool refreshing showers of rain ; but as you lead a regular tropical life, you do not feel the heat half as much, really, as in Western Australia in the summer, where people try to live an English life, notwithstanding the great heat and want of tropical appliances.

There are very good gharries, or little broughams, with venetian blinds, drawn by capital ponies, holding two people comfortably, and three at a pinch, with a picturesque driver on the box or shafts ; any number of good rickshaws, holding one person generally, with fine trotting coolies, who seem to vie with each other as to the pace they should go ; the roads are good, the scenery towards the country and the mainland of Johore most interesting to a visitor ; and the pretty houses and villas perched up on every available eminence gave us a most favourable impression.

The Government House, built by the late Sir Harry Ord, R.E., when Governor in 1869-70, is a very handsome building standing on a hill outside the city in a large, well laid-out park, with the race-course below, and we were most sumptuously entertained by Sir Cecil Smith and his charming family after their return from the visit they had been making to Penang and Malacca—his government including these places ; besides protecting native States and Johore—and he is also Consul-General for Brunei, in Borneo.

Our officers were scattered about in the numerous forts and islands which protect Singapore and the Straits; it is very strongly fortified—the works were commenced, I believe, by Major McCallum, R.E., C.M.G., in Sir William Jervois' term of government, and completed by Sir Charles Warren, who had under him my old friends Alexander, who had just left early in 1893, and Chard, V.C., who had lately come out from England.

The artillery are at the old Indian fort, Canning, in the town, the guns of which command the port. There are Asiatic (or as we used to call them) Lascar gunners in picturesque uniform attached to the R.A. for tropical work. The infantry regiments at Tanglin barracks, quite in the country, was very well off for comfortable accommodation. The barracks, commenced by Colonel Lovell in 1866, I think, were completed by Colonel Moysey in 1869-70, and I slept a night in his charming quarters in 1871 on my way home from China. The site is most picturesque, and, I believe, they are very healthy.

There are very strong bodies of native police—Sikhs, Malays, &c.—with English superintendents and superior officers to overawe the Chinamen, of whom there are about 100,000. They are well armed and drilled, and have been employed against some of the rebellious protected States; it is very necessary with the sort of hybrid population, principally Chinese, who used to get up faction fights, to be ready for any emergency.

The Government offices, Town Hall, &c., are very fine, large buildings, and we witnessed a most excellent performance of the "Mikado" there two days after we arrived. It was certainly a very hot night, but the surroundings reminded one of Japan. There were several ships of war, English and foreign, in the anchorage opposite the town; these added much to the festivity of the place, as their officers were always going to or getting up entertainments, and it seemed to us that people were never dull in this equatorial station. The clubs, banks, shops, stores, &c., are very good, and the native Chinese town, which we visited one night, all lit up for some festival, was most fairylike and romantic in appearance.

It was quite refreshing after our three weeks' voyage to have a short week, which was about our time, on shore; but as Sir Charles Warren wanted to go up to Bangkok, in Siam, and we had arranged to go with him, there was nothing for it but to say farewell to hospitable Singapore, which we should certainly like to visit again if we can manage to go on to Java, Borneo, &c., on our next tour in this part of the world.

I hear that all the old Dutch settlements are most interesting; but as you cannot see everything, we thought the kingdom of Siam would be the best place to go to.

While I am on this question I may remark we were fortunate enough to take all the money we wanted in English sovereigns, which a bank manager in Western Australia had recommended me to do, so that instead of paying 2 per cent. for bank bills or drafts, I got in exchange for our sovereigns 7½ dollars up to 8 in different parts of China, as the exchange was going down every day. The normal value of £1 being 5 dollars, I found we were really comparatively affluent, and I would recommend intending travellers to follow our example and always have about £100 in English sovereigns, using local banks when necessary only for drafts on England.

Early on the morning of 3rd February, 1893, we left in the s.s. *Hecuba* for Bangkok with Sir Charles Warren and his staff officer. There were several other passengers besides ourselves, and we had every available cabin filled. Sir Charles slept in a sort of mosquito house on the upper deck (a very necessary institution in this climate). We had a very nice attentive captain, and a fairly good table, kept for those who did not suffer from *mal-de-mer*.

For two days and nights after we left Singapore we rolled about most cheerfully. These steamers are built rather flat-bottomed, so that they can cross the bar of the river Menam, going up to Bangkok in about ten to twelve feet of water without discharging cargo.

Coming down stream from Bangkok they only fill up their holds with rice, &c., at the island outside the bar, called Koh-si-Chang, which the French took lately as their base of operations.

The cost of our passages to Bangkok was 120 dollars, or say £16 10s. at the current exchange, and as we arrived off Paknam on 6th February at 9 p.m., but did not get up to Bangkok until about 11 a.m. next day, our expenses were about 10 dols. a day, which is what we calculated all steamer expenses in this part of the world amount to, which is not out of the way for the accommodation you get—very fair cooking and plenty of room.

I see by my notes, however, that we paid only 210 dols. for our passages in a rice steamer, owned by a Chinese trading firm, from Bangkok to Hong Kong. This voyage took nearly 10 days, also including our detention at Koh-si-Chang, which I will describe later on.

At the anchorage off Paknam we found H.M.S. *Impérieuse*,

the flagship of Sir E. Fremantle, the Admiral on the China station. He himself had gone up in his despatch boat *Firebrand* with officers of the squadron to Bangkok to give the Siamese people a treat and also to play cricket, dance, ride about the place, and thoroughly enjoy their visit to this Venice of the East. The river is a very winding one from Paknam (strongly fortified in Siamese fashion) to the anchorage off the Legations and Consulates at Bangkok, and it takes, I think, two hours to go a very few miles. There are native canals for cutting off corners, but they are of no use for large steamers. There is a very good foreign hotel at Bangkok, which was very full when we arrived, as the officers of the *Impérieuse* and others occupied nearly all the rooms. However, we proceeded to interview the Minister Resident, Captain H. M. Jones, V.C., an old Crimean officer, who was very kind and hospitable, and we spent the greater part of the day with him, he taking us in his boat to see all the temples, called "wats," and principal objects of interest along the river and canals which intersect the whole place.

The houses, which are generally built on piles, line all the banks, and you can see right through them as you pass in boats; the people all seemed contented and happy, smoked a great deal, and drank the muddy waters of the river—anything but a wholesome process, and no wonder cholera is about. There was a farewell ball at the club to the Admiral and officers the night we arrived, and early next morning they left in the *Firebrand* to join the *Impérieuse* below the bar, where the admiral entertained all the *élite* of Bangkok society at a farewell lunch, &c., before he started for Singapore.

We remained in Bangkok to see what we could of the king's palace and other interesting buildings, and were most kindly invited by the Consul and his charming wife to dine and drive about with them in a most sporting pony cart, and we visited other temples, heard the king's excellent band play in the square near the palace, saw some of the soldiers at drill—their instructors and superior officers as well as their commodore and officers of their navy being "Danes," as they thought that no European complication could take place with regard to Denmark. This was before the French imbroglio; what has been done since I am not aware, but they had some good ships.

We saw the white elephants, which are rather a dirty brown colour and not particularly clean, and we thought the interior of the royal palace rather tawdry, in somewhat European style; but we were not, of course, allowed to penetrate into the private apartments. The king was supposed to be indisposed and unable to entertain, and I doubt if even the Admiral saw him.

The coinage of the country is silver, in little "ticals," which are something in value between a franc and a shilling, as far as I can remember; but it is rather a difficult calculation when you come to pay a bill in "ticals"—with dollars at a discount.

Sir Charles Warren wanted to go on to Ayuthia, the ancient capital up the river, where the sacred elephants, &c., are kept, but as this involved a day's journey in a steam launch, a stay there, and another journey back, we decided to take ship on the third day and proceed towards Hong Kong as we had arranged, there being a very nice little steamer called the *Phra-Chula-Clum-Klao*, which is one of the royal family names, and in which we made a most comfortable voyage, lasting nearly ten days.

After bidding farewell to our friends, wiring to England *viâ* Burmah, and interviewing the bank manager—a very important person in your travels—we dropped down the river to Paknam, where we had to wait near Mosquitoe Point for the tide to rise sufficiently to take us over the bar. The mosquitoes here are really too fearful; you can hardly eat your food or sit down for a moment; they get inside nets and are generally a pest, and the French must have suffered awfully the summer they were blockading Bangkok. We had met their admiral (Humann) and his flag captain several times in China, and we pitied them for what we knew they had in store when they left Nagasaki in June, 1893, for Siam.

However, everything comes to an end, and we eventually crossed the bar and made for the beautiful island Koh-si-Chang, where we filled up our steamer with rice for China.

On this island, which is hilly, well-wooded, and comparatively cool, the King of Siam was building a sort of marine retreat to supersede a temporary mat shed erection which he kept for summer use, the idea being that when politics got too warm in his capital, he should take himself and his family far away from the "busy hum of men" and enjoy the *dolce-far-niente* of repose, and "lotus" and "betel nut" eating. Alas, the French were too many for him, and Admiral Humann took it for his depôt some months later. There were many other steamers here loading up for China, &c., and the king's steam yacht, commanded by his pet commodore, arrived just before we left on 11th February;

she was a smart-looking craft, and, I believe, fairly fast. The king had also a large modern steamer, like a small ironclad, at Bangkok, in which he was very anxious to visit England, but there were complications which prevented him. After leaving Koh-si-Chang you pass many islands off the coast of Siam and Cambodia, with fine mountains in the distance on the mainland, until you make Cape Cambodia, the south-west point of French Cochin China. There are several islets off the coast which, I should say, make the navigation difficult, but our little captain—a most courteous Irishman—seemed to know the coast by intuition; he was always going up and down the China Sea and Gulf of Siam, and he nearly always seemed to be on the bridge.

We had most excellent accommodation—rather like a yacht—a small saloon stretching across the deck amidships, with about half a dozen cabins aft; a nice little poop, sufficient for gentle exercise; a capital cook; piano and other luxuries; and fine weather. I think the steamer was under 1,000 tons, but rather larger than the *Hecuba*, in which we journeyed from Singapore to Bangkok.

There are, I understand, a good many German steamers on this line also, but the Chinese line was the best fitted for passengers, and we certainly had no reason to complain.

After passing Cape Cambodia you draw up north, passing the entrance to the river Mekong, on which Saigon, the French capital of Cochin China, is situated, and make the fine lighthouse off Cape St. Jacques, when you go still more north, skirting the coast of Anam, which is also protected by the French. One night the whole of the ridge of hills or mountains along the shore was lit up as for an illumination; there seemed to be miles of flame, but the captain explained that they were simply burning the woods —to improve the pastures or grass, I suppose—which seemed to be rather a reckless proceeding.

There is an enormous amount of rice exported from Siam, Saigon and Cochin China, generally to Hong Kong, to help to support the Chinese.

When you have reached about latitude 15° north, you make across the China Sea for Hong Kong, which takes you about three days only out of sight of land. This may, therefore, be described as another yachting voyage. Nearing Hong Kong you get among an archipelago of islands, which, if the weather is clear, is doubtless very picturesque; but, unfortunately, we got into our usual fog here, and the captain had to be most careful until we could sight the nearest lighthouse to Hong Kong Island, on 18th February, when we slipped in through the Green Island passage, west of Hong Kong, to the anchorage off the city, which I had not seen since 1871—twenty-two years. It was very cold, and the winter had been the most severe for fifty years (which is about the time we took the place), but I received a most friendly letter from Col. Mulloy, C.R.E., who was expecting me, and we landed in a steam launch at the Hong Kong Hotel.

Unfortunately, we had left all our heavy baggage, with our thick clothes, at Singapore, to be forwarded afterwards, and the result was that we were shivering in semi-tropical garments for a few days in a China winter, which we had not really anticipated would be so severe. I believe it was the first time some of the Chinamen in Hong Kong had seen ice on the "Peak."

IV.

The first thing that strikes a visitor to Hong Kong is, I think, that it is a beautiful city and a most picturesque island. My introduction to it, in 1868, from the deck of a P. & O. steamer on a summer's night, with all the lights twinkling up the hill and sides of the "Peak," was most pleasing; now electric light all over the place, and immense improvements in the streets and public buildings, made the place doubly interesting to my wife and myself, who had not seen it for twenty-two years.

The houses, which in our time only reached about 400 feet above the sea, are now thickly built almost up to the "Gap," at least 1,000 feet higher, and many beautiful hotels, houses, bungalows and clubs are established in the punchbowl, or extinct crater, which is cool all the year round, the only disadvantage being that it is damp and often in the clouds; but when it does clear, the views of the harbour on one side, and the neighbouring islands and ocean on the other, are most fascinating.

The cable "tram" or railway takes you up most comfortably in about ten minutes from the station just above the Cathedral and Murray Barracks; many pretty houses are situated on the road, and the whole life of the place is altered by this mountain residence.

The "Peak" towers grandly over all. Opposite, on the mainland of China, the town and military station of Kowloon have increased enormously in size since 1871.

The Hong Kong Regiment, a very fine body of men, raised in India for service in China, have their barracks and cantonment there; the garrison musketry practice is carried out on the peninsula; and numerous docks, stores and warehouses make it a most busy place. There is also the Government observatory—a most important object for time and weather.

I do not propose to go much into detail about this part of our travels, as there are many of our officers and others in China who can describe the place much more graphically than it is possible for me to do; but as our object was to get up to Pekin, Japan, and as far north as might be, and return to Hong Kong, with a view to going down south to the eastern side of Australia before the weather got too hot, we limited our stay in Hong Kong to three weeks, which enabled us to see and do nearly everything in reason.

It was supposed to be the season of Lent when we arrived, but the races took place the next week, and everyone woke up to the fact that it was necessary to be seen on the race-course at least two days out of three.

The regiments and clubs had stands and lunches "galore" —we were most hospitably entertained by the Shropshires, the R.A. and R.E.—and the "grand stand" presented a galaxy of beauty and costume. The racing was not much to see—principally ponies—and betting was strictly forbidden. I believe there was a "totalizator" under club management, but the Chinamen, who love gambling, were apparently not allowed to participate; and I think the natives took much less interest in the matter than when I can remember them in 1868-70.

"The soldiers" usually found one or two excellent jockeys, and I can number among my friends several distinguished officers who commenced their racing career on the old "Happy Valley" race-course of Hong Kong.

Curiously enough, the weather was too cold for perfect enjoyment. We seldom saw the sun, and as there was a nasty raw feeling in the air we managed to get chilled more than once, and had to be very careful in our movements.

The Governor, Sir William Robinson, K.C.M.G. (no relation of the Governor of Western Australia), and his family were most kind and hospitable; he was a very active man, playing lawn tennis, and going in hard for everything.

The General, G. D. Barker, and his family were most friendly and courteous. The R.E. there, under Colonel Molloy, with my friends Bennet, Dumbleton, McCarthy, and others, did everything to make our stay pleasant. The R.E. Mess in Queen's Gardens—I think it is called—had only to be known to be appreciated. The views from the verandah of these charming houses over the harbour and mouth of the Canton river were most picturesque, and the Ladies' "Lawn Tennis" Club near was a great attraction.

The Hong Kong Hotel was very comfortable; our corner rooms on the third floor had a magnificent look-out.

A few of my old friends in the Civil Service, Banks, Jardine, Matheson & Co., and other mercantile houses, were very hospitable. We dined and lunched out frequently. We also found pleasant acquaintances in the navy, many ships being in harbour re-fitting for new commissions.

We went up to Canton in the fine river steamer *Powan*,

passing the Bogue Forts, Bocca-Tigris, and other places well known to our forces in early Chinese wars, now again heavily armed and garrisoned, judging by the number of guns and banners we saw displayed.

Canton looked, if anything, dirtier and smelt worse than I remembered it in former days, and being about Chinese New-Year time, the people were more truculent and disagreeable in manner than usual; and after visiting some curio shops, temples, dining, and going to a German fancy ball at the club on Shameen Island, the English concession, where nearly all the foreigners live, we returned to our steamer, which had most comfortable cabins, and early the next morning steamed down to Hong Kong by Whampoa and other well-known places, arriving late in the afternoon.

We ought to have gone to Macao (Portuguese), where I had been before, Manila (Spanish), and other ports, which you can get at most easily, but we decided to put ourselves on board the s.s. *Hai-loong*, bound for Swatow, Amoy, and Foochow, on the 8th March, when the weather was beginning to get warmer and we did see the sun.

It is very pretty going out of Hong Kong by the narrow Lye-e-Moon Pass to the east and north, well fortified now at every available point, and, I believe, well defended by submarine mines, and a most difficult passage for an opposed enemy to force.

The other passage from the westward by Green Island is not so tortuous, but is also well defended.

We arrived at Swatow early on 9th March—found a great deal of trade and business going on; steamers loading, &c., bean-cake being the greatest export. We lunched with the British Consul, Mr. Wilkinson, who we found had exploited the game of "Khanhoo" or Chinese whist, which we had been playing all the way out from England, a capital amusement for three or four people, which had enabled us to pass many hours on wet and dull days most agreeably. The game can be bought at the Stores.

Swatow had also a charm for me because of my first visit, early in 1869, when I had been employed with a naval brigade, under Commodore Oliver J. Jones, R.N., in suppressing piracy on the river Han between Swatow and Chao-Chao-Fu, the treaty port of the province, which has enabled trade to be carried on peacefully ever since, where formerly it was most dangerous, the river Han pirates being proverbial in this part of China for ferocity and rapine.

We reached Amoy on 10th March. Passed a very pleasant morning with some old friends on the island of Kiu-lan-su, where the English and foreign community generally live, a very picturesque and healthy place, which we had visited frequently in 1869-70; and on 11th March arrived at the White Dogs, and thence up to the Pagoda anchorage in the river Min, among most beautiful scenery—being called the Rhine of China—and then in a steam launch to the city of Foochow, ten miles off, the river here being very shallow in places. At Fow-Chow we spent two days with Mr. Graham, the representative of Messrs. Jardine, Matheson & Company, who have a most palatial house here. We were most hospitably entertained. Attended Divine Service in the pretty church near the settlement; saw the race course, where much pony racing, lawn tennis, and cricket are done; went in a boat up the river Min to see the long stone bridge which connects the city with the foreign settlement; visited the club for afternoon tea, &c.

Fow-Chow, like many other Chinese cities, is surrounded by native cemeteries, in which numerous tombstones and tablets abound. There is great difficulty often in making roads and paths and clearing sites for houses without buying up all the family ancestral rights, about which the Chinese are very jealous. There are many monasteries also here.

I am very sorry to see the news from this place of the massacre of the missionaries at Ku-Chang lately; but I fear they will always be liable to these outbreaks until the corrupt Government is reformed.

We joined our new steamer, the China merchants' *Hai-Shin*, at Pagoda anchorage on night of 13th March, and dropped down the river early next morning, *en route* to Shanghai. I see that our passages from Hong Kong to Shanghai cost us 180 dollars, which would be, as I said before, about ten dollars a day each for six days.

Formerly, when at Fow-Chow and Amoy in 1869-70, I had gone over to Formosa with some friends, to the northern port, Tam-Sui, with its adjacent port and coal mines of Keelung, being only about 100 miles from Fow-Chow, and Taku, the southern port, near Taiwan-Foo, the capital, about the same distance from Amoy. We were nearly swamped on the bar at Taku in 1869; there is always a nasty sea, which put out our gunboat engine-room fires, and we only had just sufficient steam on to "wobble" into the perfectly safe harbour.

The island of Formosa is, no doubt, very beautiful in parts. The Dutch had a settlement near Amping centuries ago, but the Chinese have never thoroughly exploited it, as the mountainous interior is supposed to be inhabited by savages who have never been subdued. The Japanese will not have an easy task even now to conquer the island. In the good old gunboat days, between 1860 and 1870, it was not unusual for a lieutenant, with nearly all his crew—boatswain, gunner, twenty men, and a field-gun—to take possession of some of the Chinese seaport towns on the island, and hold them to ransom until compensation was paid for outrage on British subjects—a very simple way of settling matters.

In the Formosa Channel, between the island and the mainland, the P. & O. steamer *Bok-hara* had been lost in a typhoon the previous winter, 1892, on the Pescadores, a dangerous group of islands near, and nearly all on board were drowned.

I see by my notes that we sighted Chusan Island early on 15th March. We have occupied it as a military station more than once during Chinese wars, and it always seemed to me a great pity to give it up, as it commands the approaches to Ningpo and Shanghai, and is a very central point, both for ships and men. I suppose that international jealousy would prevent our taking it at the present juncture, but with the Japanese in Formosa, we ought to have another island.

We anchored for the night at Woosung, where the Chinese have forts and batteries which seemed to be firing salutes or practising all night. Early in the morning of 16th March we went up to Shanghai, which is considered the "Model Settlement" of European China.

The buildings in the English "concession" are doubtless very fine, and the government by a foreign municipality also successful; but the native Chinese city is dirty and smelly to a degree, and one avoids it as much as possible.

We stayed at the Astor House Hotel, more or less run by Americans, across the well-known bridge over the Soochow creek, and were very comfortable, although they were rebuilding and repairing the hotel. The Consul-General, Mr. (now Sir) N. T. Hannen, and his family were most kind and attentive, driving us about, showing us the many sights, and on St. Patrick's Day we had a concert and dance at the splendid club, supposed to be nearly the best in the East. We saw the volunteer force, cavalry, artillery and infantry, drilling on the racecourse—a most creditable performance—and we paid several visits on the "Bubbling-well" road, where there is also a very pretty club *à la* Hurlingham. Several men-of-war, English and foreign, were anchored off the "bund," but H.M.S. *Severn* was the best specimen of a fast cruiser; the French Admiral was also here. The Chinese had several ships here and at Woosung, but there was a good deal of what one calls in this part of the world "look see pigeon" about them.

After a rather short week at Shanghai, we decided to start in one of the fine river steamers—called *Poyang* — to Hankow, about 600 miles up the Yang-tze-kiang, one of the largest rivers in the world. We left Shanghai early on the 22nd March; reached Ching-kiang that night. There was a great deal of rain, and we did not land. We passed Nankin, now a most decayed city, the next day, arriving at Wuhu, another treaty port, that night. The next afternoon arrived at Kiu-Kiang, and on the 25th, about noon, reached Hankow. Here we found an English man-of-war, the *Porpoise*, an American, and two large Russian gun-boats with their admiral, which were anchored off the bund of the foreign settlement, a most interesting place as an evidence of the enterprise and energy of the foreign community: fine buildings, well-laid-out gardens, racecourse, golf ground, &c., almost in the middle of China. There is a great "divide" of the river here, and the more northerly branch runs for hundreds of miles towards Mongolia. The main river runs on past the Tong-ting lake to Ichang, a treaty port, where the gun-boat *Esk* was stationed, commanded by Lieutenant Ravenhill, R.N., to Kwei-chow and Chung-King, the latter being also an inland treaty port, where we have a consul, and so on through Yunan almost to Bhamo. I only mention these places to show what an immense river this Yang-tze is, and the rise and fall at Hankow is something like fifty feet between summer and winter levels. No wonder they have to provide a most efficient "bund" or wharf, and the variety of climate is also extreme. There is a Chinese arsenal, &c., at Hankow on one side of the river, and a cotton mill owned by the Viceroy, with splendid machinery, on the other side.

I do not propose to describe the river more in detail, as so many books have been written on the subject; Blakiston and Laurence Oliphant, about the time of the last Chinese War, gave most graphic descriptions, and General Yule and poor Gill, in later days, made the public acquainted with the upper reaches of the Yang-tze. We decided not to go on to Ichang—to which smaller, but good steamers run from Hankow—as there is always a chance of being "detained" on a sandbank, and we had not a week to spare to do the second trip. I was very sorry, as the scenery about the Ichang gorges is, I believe, very fine; we had pictures of them, which made us long to go on and judge for ourselves. However, after two days at Hankow, we returned in the same steamer (*Poyang*), with its genial Captain Perks, to Shanghai, stopping at the same ports going down, and visiting most of the hospitable consuls *en route*.

The only picturesque portion is between Kiu-Kiang and Wuhu, where the Orphans' Rock and passes are very interesting, with a temple and monastery perched high above the river on this solitary little island.

All the country between Nankin and Shanghai is more or less sacred to Charlie Gordon and his "Ever-Victorious Army," and when you see what fearful devastation was committed by the Taipings in what was formerly a most thriving and densely-populated province, you wonder at the power of recuperation of the Chinese. They are a most thrifty and hard-working race.

We returned to Shanghai on 30th March, and, as it was the day before Good Friday, everyone was preparing for the Easter Holidays.

I found my friend Colonel Henry Robinson, R.E., who was "globe-trotting," staying here, *en route* to Japan—we had met him in Hong Kong previously—and a Colonel Hughes Hallett, Judge-Advocate-General from Madras, who was making an exhaustive tour in China. He was off to Nankin to study Chinese "military law." I see by my notes it was very wet at this time, and as we wanted to get on to Pekin, we took passage on 1st April in the s.s. *Hsin-Yu*, owned by a Chinese company, to go *viâ* Chefoo to Tientsin, for which we paid 165 dols. She was supposed to be the fastest steamer of the line, and we had most comfortable cabins, an excellent table, and very few passengers; and early on Easter Sunday morning we started for the north, after saying farewell to our many hospitable friends.

We reached Chefoo—a treaty port a short distance beyond Wei-hai-wei, which has lately been captured by the Japanese—on 4th April; but it was blowing too hard in the open roadstead to land comfortably, and as we had to return this way, we did not mind. We left Chefoo on the night of 5th April, crossed the bar at Taku near the forts on 6th April, and reached Tientsin—the treaty port for Pekin—the same night, after an exciting passage up the narrow Pei-ho River, for junks and boats were constantly coming down.

The forts and batteries at Taku and its neighbourhood seem to have been re-built and re-armed recently. The Chinese Government, or, I suppose, Li Hung Chang, the Viceroy, was building a new battery, when we passed, and there were many signs of careful preparations for war, although at the time we were in China we heard nothing of any Japanese difficulty.

On the 7th April, 1893, we spent the early part of the day at Tientsin, making arrangements to go up the Peiho to Pekin, if possible that afternoon, as we were pressed for time. I called on Mr. Brenan, the Consul, an old acquaintance, and other people to whom I had introductions, and Mr. Dettring, the head of the Chinese Customs, kindly promised his steam launch to tow us as far as possible. We hired a house-boat—which had apparently been used previously by some Mandarin—at a cost of about 50 dols.; this included all the crew and their keep. I engaged an experienced old Chinese "boy," and the hotel-keeper at the Astor House supplied a capital cook and provisions for about a week; we put our baggage on board, including my excellent chair, and about 3.15 p.m. left the wharf *en route* to the capital, and were towed for about twelve miles by the Customs launch, which was of great service to us.

The house-boat had two rooms, one of which was our dining and drawing room, and my bedroom at night; I slept on the table, the "boy" in a small ante-room forward, and the ladies had the bedroom further aft. The crew, when they were not trimming sails, poling, tracking on the banks, or eating their "chow-chow," were stowed somewhere underneath; they appeared and disappeared at mysterious times, and were about twelve in number with the skipper and his mate.

It took us from Friday, 7th, to early on Monday, 10th, to reach Tungchow, which is the head of the practicable navigation of the Peiho River—about 120 miles by water, poling, towing, and sailing where possible. I celebrated my fifty-fifth birthday on board, and we had quite a festivity on 8th April.

We read, wrote letters, played "khanhoo," and admired the rather dull scenery for two whole days, usually anchoring at night, and occasionally getting aground and sticking on the sand banks. We passed many junks sailing or being towed from the bank of the river, and near Ho-si-wu we saw hundreds of the Imperial salt junks laid up for the season, having conveyed this tribute to Pekin, where I believe it is stored and doled out to the people at a very enhanced price. Grain is stored in the same way, and this is, I suppose, one of the "privileges" of the Imperial family, the people being impoverished accordingly. They are a queer people, and no wonder there are famines periodically.

At Tungchow—rather a large town (whence you ought to go by canal to Pekin, about fifteen miles, but as my "boy" said, in his "pidgin" English, "No can—makee mend ")—you hire carts, mules, ponies, or chairs to go to Pekin overland. You cannot call it by road, as the road, formerly paved with large stone blocks, has almost ceased to exist, and you take to the fields and go off the road—where the stones are often turned up on end—wherever you can.

The Pekin carts which we hired are of a "sealed pattern" description : no springs, very strong shafts, and body in one piece, the strongest axle and almost solid wheels, drawn by ponies or mules, and only large enough to hold one person uncomfortably. We had five in our solemn procession, three for ourselves, one for the "boy," and one for the baggage, and we bumped about, either riding on the shaft beside the driver, or reclining under the awnings, until we got out and walked in desperation. It is an awful five hours' journey. You cross the river at Palikao, where the English and the French fought an action with the Chinese in 1860, and from which General Montauban took his title of Count. There is a fine stone bridge there still, with some of the ornaments or figures knocked off by our guns, which have never been replaced.

We lunched half-way in a pretty wood, and caught sight of Pekin about 3 p.m., the country being slightly undulating. You seem to see the huge towers and walls all at once ; they look like the pictures in story books of the East, and probably existed in the time of Marco Polo and Genghis Khan.

You enter through one of the numerous towers or gateways with a slovenly guard looking on, who, as far as I know, exacts "backsheesh" or a "squeeze" from your "boy" for the privilege of passing. There were crowds of people going in and out, riding, walking, being carried in chairs or carts ;

and strings of camels coming in from Mongolia added something picturesque to the scene.

I do not propose to describe Pekin, which has been done by many better writers, but only to notice what we saw. It is a city within a city, a sort of key-pattern puzzle place, with the Imperial palace in the centre, the Imperial city, the Tartar city, and so forth outside. A stranger never gets near the Imperial part except to look at the entrance. If you stop any time, more particularly with ladies, admiring objects, you are liable to be surrounded by a curious mob, whose Chinese perfume is not that of "Araby the blest."

We stayed at the Foreign Hotel, which was run by a French storekeeper and his family, where we had most excellent cooking and fair accommodation. It was very full, and among the guests were a London solicitor and his wife, who had just come back from a three days' trip to the Ming Tombs and Great Wall; a retired Indian civilian traveller, who was starting for the Kara-Koram mountains and thence overland through Russia home—he made a most interesting journey, the account of which I have read since; two young Englishmen who were travelling round the world, and who had ridden up from Tientsin overland, leaving the day after us. There was a French gentleman and his friend also from Alsace, all of whom eventually, with the exception of the Indian civilian, accompanied us in the steamer from Tientsin to Japan.

We were most hospitably received by our Minister, Mr. (now Sir) N. R. O'Conor, K.C.B., and his charming wife, and we were present at the Legation at a large party, when "Box and Cox" was played, and we danced afterwards until the small hours. We met nearly all the Corps Diplomatique at the Legation, which is a beautiful old palace standing in a compound or park, kept in admirable order, quite a contrast to the dirt and untidiness of the roads and streets outside. All the Ministers and Chinese high officials have these yamens or palaces nearly always surrounded by gardens with ornamented walls and gateways, which cover a great deal of ground, and cause Pekin to look such a large city when viewed from the walls. It is about a day's journey round.

I was unable to see Sir Robert Hart, the Inspector-General of Chinese Customs, as he was unwell. There had been a great deal of festivity just before our arrival on account of the farewells to the German Minister, who was leaving, after about thirty years' service in China, to get married and retire into private life in Europe. Most of the Legations had been entertaining their popular colleague, and it was like the end of the London season, getting rather hot, and people were worn out with gaiety. Dr. Dudgeon, the medical officer to the Chinese Customs, however, was most kind and attentive; he took us over the principal sights of Pekin: temples, where possible to be seen, observatory, city walls, and introduced me to the Anamese ambassadors. Dr. Dudgeon had been about a quarter of a century in Pekin, and was much respected by natives and foreigners; he could speak the language most fluently, and was, therefore, an excellent guide. There is a great deal of sight-seeing to be done, curios to be bought, and possibly money to be made; but the smells, dirt, and disagreeables of the city, in my humble opinion, outweigh the pleasures of visiting this extraordinary place; the people are uncivil, and the feeling against foreigners was certainly bad when we were there.

We left Pekin again on the afternoon of the 13th April, reached Tungchow late that evening, and went on board our house-boat, which, at all events, was very clean, and we reached Tientsin after two days down stream, on the night of 15th April, very glad indeed to return to the Astor House Hotel.

I calculate that our expenses in Pekin were about 65 dols., and the cost of provisioning the boat about 45 dols.; so that with fees to the "boy," cook, and boatmen (who always try to get more than their contract), our trip to Pekin cost us 170 dollars.

We spent Sunday, 16th April, very pleasantly in Tientsin, and it was beautiful weather.

There is a nice little church, and a tolerably large European and American community. We had friends to see, letters to write, and paid a visit to the Consulate at tea-time. Nearly all the principal buildings are situated on the Peiho River, with shops, stores, and some pretty houses in the back and cross streets. There is a public garden and a town band of Chinese, who discoursed excellent music on the Monday. There is, of course, a club where the residents make you very much "at home," and there is a very large Chinese city to see if you are so inclined. There is another large river called Yunho, which joins the Peiho here, and a great junk trade is apparently thriving, for the river wharves are crowded with native boats, and everyone seems busy and prosperous.

The Viceroy, Li Hung Chang, now an old man—formerly Charlie Gordon's friend—and supposed to be the most powerful and influential official in China, lives in the city in a fine palace, and is very polite and hospitable to the

Europeans. Unfortunately, our time did not admit of being present at one of his "at home" days, and I had to depend upon the British Consul's information for current topics and politics. There is a large French Roman Catholic Cathedral here, built on the site of that destroyed by the Chinese rioters in 1870, when they murdered the French Consul and some Sisters of Charity; the building is now the most conspicuous object at the turn of the river, and I believe it is a very sore subject with the Chinese that they had to rebuild this memorial to their own cruelty and perfidy. I was travelling in H.M.S. *Adventure* up to Shanghai at the time of the massacre, and it was then thought that it might spread to the treaty ports, and every available man-of-war and steamer was sent up to Tientsin from the south.

We met Captain von Hanneken, of the German artillery, at dinner at the Consulate the night before we left Tientsin. He was an extremely agreeable, well-informed officer, who was then going home to get some more Krupp guns, it was generally supposed, although his time of service with the Chinese Government had expired; but, as we know now, he has since returned, and narrowly escaped being killed in more that one naval engagement with the Japanese. He was a brave man, but I think had little influence with the Chinese.

We took our passages in the Japanese s.s. *Genkai-Maru*, on the 17th April, for Chefoo, the Corea and Japan, for which we paid 180 dols.—somewhere about £24, according to the then exchange—for a ten days' voyage, which was very reasonable; and she was a most comfortable steamer, nearly all the officers and crew, with the exception of the captain, the first and second mates, being Japanese, even the chief engineer, who had graduated in Glasgow. The large Japanese steamship company who owned this steamer and many others found nearly all the transports in the recent war with China.

We left the wharf early on the 18th April, but had considerable difficulty in turning round, the river being so narrow here. We dropped down to Taku, and after waiting some little time for the tide and more cargo, crossed the bar in the afternoon, and at 7 p.m. the next day arrived at Chefoo, too late to land.

We spent the next morning, 20th April, with the hospitable Consul, who took us over the principal sights in this pretty place, which is the chief bathing and summer resort of many families from the southern ports, which are much hotter. There is a capital beach and many nice houses and hotels. During the late war it was the naval rendezvous for our fleet and others during the operations in the Gulf of Pecheli.

Port Arthur, opposite, near Talien-Whan-Bay, where our Pekin expedition assembled in 1860, and Wei-hai-Wei, between Chefoo and the Shantung promontory, make Chefoo a very important place. We found the son of an old friend here, also in the Imperial Chinese Customs, and we lunched with him and his bride in a very pretty bungalow overlooking the harbour. There are, in fact, two bays, with a fine promontory—where the lighthouse and Consulates are situated—dividing them. We had a long conversation with an English naval lieutenant, who had come in from Wei-hai-Wei in a Chinese gunboat for a little change. He was then gunnery instructor, and the last of the European officers employed in the Chinese service; they had carefully got rid of nearly everyone likely to be useful to them in case of war.

We left Chefoo that evening and had a fine passage to Chemulpo, in Corea, on the west side of that very peculiar kingdom. It is the nearest port to Seoul, the capital, but time did not permit of our going overland in chairs twenty miles, or round by the river in a steam launch, which went at irregular intervals, and we should have had to wait for another steamer. It is a very picturesque harbour, with many islands and promontories in its neighbourhood.

There was a Japanese despatch vessel in the harbour, which was said to do twenty knots uncomfortably, built, I think, by themselves, with engines from England. They say she "jumped" tremendously when going full speed. The Vice-Consul came off and gave us all the news; there was an incipient rebellion going on at Seoul, and all the foreign drilled troops near Chemulpo were being drafted to Seoul to defend the king's palace. I believe they were a very ragged army, more or less instructed by Americans.

One of our passengers, a sort of Scotch-American, went overland to Seoul, and his description of the place afterwards did not seem to be favourable enough to induce other people to go. It was described to me as a miniature Pekin, surrounded by hills which excluded the air, and the dirt and smells were worse than in China proper. We shifted our anchorage in the evening, and lay so far from shore that it was with considerable difficulty anyone got off to the steamer.

There was an American man-of-war here also, and an English one came in before we left.

Just before we went to Corea, the German Minister at Pekin had been there to marry the daughter of the American Consul-General at Seoul—another friend of ours—and we were very sorry that we had not timed our visit a fortnight earlier, but we did not know of it soon enough to alter our arrangements, but only saw the minister on his steamer crossing the bar at "Taku" as we were going up to Tientsin and he was coming down the river.

We had on board the Chinese Secretary of the German Embassy at Pekin, a very nice reserve officer, who was going on leave to Japan. He had been several years in China, and was an accomplished linguist.

We left Chemulpo on the afternoon of the 22nd April, and coasted round the Corean promontory, sighting Port Hamilton (a vacated English naval station) on Sunday, 23rd April, in dull, cool weather, and rather inclined to blow, and early on the 24th we arrived at Fusan, a port in the S.E. end of Corea, where there is a very good harbour, used occasionally by the Russians as a coaling station, and by ourselves. Fusan is an extraordinary place in many ways, for here the Japanese have established a port (with or without treaty) and keep the Coreans out of their town at night, only allowing them to do business in the day-time; much as we do in Canton by treaty. There is a good deal of bean-cake trade here and in other parts of Corea, and the Commissioner of Chinese Customs seemed a busy man, although his office was in the Japanese and not in the Corean town, which was some distance off. We had a disagreeable adventure in a small ship's boat going off to the steamer in the afternoon, for it came on to blow and we were gradually being driven out to sea, and had to be rescued by a cargo boat from the steamer—being pretty well drenched with rain and spray.

We left Fusan that evening, and after a terrible night of pitching and rolling in the straights between Corea and Japan, we reached the coast near Hirado Island, and getting into smooth water, entered the lovely land-locked harbour of Nagasaki on the afternoon of the 25th April.

This was my second visit to Japan, for I had been invalided there from Hong Kong in 1870, but to my wife and daughter their first impressions of Japan were most favourable, and I think Nagasaki is really one of the most beautiful places we have ever seen.

V.

WE found H.M.S. *Leander*, the French flagship *Triomphante* (celebrated as Pierre Loti's temporary abode when writing Madame Chrysanthème about this very place, Nagasaki), a Russian man-of-war, Japanese, and others in the harbour. It had been blowing so hard the previous night, 24th April, that some of the men-of-war had dragged their anchors and drifted about cheerfully. The Harbour is so shut in that it seems almost impossible that it can blow here. We landed and saw many temples, bazaars, and curio shops: we called at the English Consulate and walked about this most interesting town, with its beautiful background of hills and woods; but the part that interested me most, as well as at my former visit in 1870, was the little island of houses and factories called Desima, close to the shore, where the Dutch submitted to be shut up for many years or even centuries in order that they might carry on their lucrative monopoly of trade with Japan. We English submitted to many similar indignities on the part of the Chinese by being shut out of Canton and only allowed to trade on the Honam side and the factories, until the wars of 1841 and 1857-60 opened up many treaty ports; but we were never pinched in as the Dutch allowed themselves to be, for we had Macao and Hong Kong to fall back upon, and gradually extended our influence to other places.

We were shown the island of Pappenberg going into Nagasaki, where nearly 300 years ago all the Christians then in this part of Japan were massacred by being forced to jump off the rocks into the sea. I found Lawrence Oliphant's book most interesting reading here, as he went up with Lord Elgin's mission to Yeddo—now called Tokyo —in 1858, when the country was first opened for trade to us, although the Americans had concluded a treaty with the Japanese Government some time previously. What enormous strides in civilisation and trade have taken place in thirty-five years!

We saw a good many Japanese officers and soldiers very well turned out, but the part where they fail is in their boots; they don't seem yet to have arrived at the way to wear them properly, and they are never particularly clean. There were a good many artillery in Nagasaki to man the forts and batteries. We spent the evening with Captain Castle, R.N., on board the *Leander*, and he showed us his wonderful collection of photographs of the Sandwich and South Sea Islands, which he had taken in a previous cruise. He made us long to see these beautiful places, and several months afterwards, when in Sydney, we were able to gratify our wishes, when we went in a steamer round New Caledonia, some of the New Hebrides, and Fiji. The *Leander* was being prepared to take our Minister in China and his family round the treaty ports, and Captain Castle, on hospitable thoughts intent, showed us all his excellent arrangements for their comfort. It always strikes me that sailors are very ingenious and thoughtful.

We left Nagasaki early next morning, a P. & O., North German Lloyd, and other mail steamers being close to us, and coasted round to Shimonoseki at the entrance to the Inland Sea, where we coaled and bought curios. Some of our passengers went on shore at Moji, opposite Shimonoseki, to see a prize-fight at a fair, which they described as very funny. The railways to connect with Kobé and Nagasaki were proceeding, and there seemed to be any amount of trade and business.

All this part of the coast is very picturesque. My recollection of this place is that it was very red; but the green woods, hills, and small natural harbours and bays made it most interesting. There are many lighthouses and evidences of careful navigation, considering that it is only about thirty years since we had to destroy the Japanese batteries here, as they wished to prevent our making use of the Inland Sea at all. We left about 5 p.m., but it was too late to see the most beautiful part of the Inland Sea, which we went through at night, and there was no moon. I had seen it all before, but my ladies were much disappointed at only really seeing the two ends. We arrived at Kobé on April 27th, early in the afternoon, and found many steamers, ships, and a brisk trade going on, for it is now the principal foreign port of Japan, Yokohama having dwindled down as Kobé and Hiogo, its neighbour, went up in importance.

Having said good-bye to all our steamer friends on board the *Genkai-Maru*, with whom we had passed an eventful ten days, we landed at the Custom House, where they made no difficulty except with regard to firearms, swords and kodaks, for which they charged heavy duties as they could make them all themselves, and photograph better than foreigners. Our two French friends were much troubled by their photographic apparatus being taken to the bonded store until it was released the next day.

Kobé and Hiogo, which practically join, are very large and extensive; the native town most picturesque. There are any number of temples on the hills at the back of the town and on the sea shore, and we spent our Sunday afternoon at a sweet place called Akashi, which you reach by the railway, which now extends to Hiroshima and Shimonoseki, I believe. We found many friends in Kobé, and we stayed at the Oriental Hotel, which had a capital restaurant and fairly comfortable rooms. I found at Kobé an old acquaintance and namesake, who had originally been at Hong Kong in the Naval Medical Department, but had gone up to Japan about 1870, started a dispensary and drug store, and has done very well for himself. He is a great athlete, yachtsman, steam launcher, and good "all round." His portrait adorns the hall of the Gymnastic Club, of which he was a long time president. He was very kind to us, and we had a lovely sail in his yacht in the bay. We saw the waterfalls, paid a visit to Osaka—a huge city where the new Japanese Mint (originally brought from Hong-Kong) and other public institutions are, including a fine castle and barracks, reached by railway in about an hour. We also attended a ball given at the Oriental Hotel by my friend Mr. Baggallay, and dined with him at his hospitable abode the evening before we left. The houses here are very good. There is, of course, a club, a very fine one, where they have also lawn-tennis, &c., and a capital gymnasium. The banks, insurance offices, stores, and shops in the

European settlement of Kobé are most creditable to foreign enterprise, for when I remember it in 1870 it was very primitive.

Having stayed five days in Kobé, we thought it time to move to Kyoto, a lovely old city—formerly the residence of the Mikado—in the hills, about fifty miles from Kobé, where there are two excellent hotels, usually full of visitors.

The railway journey takes some little time, as the trains are not fast, and, when we arrived, it was in pouring rain. We stayed at Yaamis' Hotel, outside the city, on the slope of a beautiful hill, with a pretty garden all round, and wide verandahs, where you could sit and admire the lovely views. Palaces, temples, curio shops, china manufactures, and bazaars make Kyoto a most interesting place for travellers. There is always something going on. We made trips to Otzu and Lake Biwa, where you go by rail or road, and return by canal through a long tunnel to a curious portage down to the river level, an engineering feat of which the Japanese are very proud. We saw one of their religious Shinto processions from the windows of a Japanese dentist's surgery, lent to us for the occasion; most picturesque, everything being white; the singing and excitement overpowering; and the high priest in a brougham behind, followed by his horse, which he had to mount later on near the temple, was most amusing—something like an indifferent end to a Lord Mayor's Show. But their temples, shrines, gardens, and woods are most fascinating. We spent a week here, meeting many friends with whom we had travelled, and others coming on from India—among them two Guardsmen from the Staff, returning home, one of them a London friend of ours. We came in only for the end of the cherry-blossom season in our travels; but found azaleas, wistarias, peonies, &c., in full bloom and most beautiful in the neighbourhood of Kyoto. One might spend a month most pleasantly here; but, as our time was limited, and we wanted to catch a good steamer from Hong Kong to Australia in June, we felt bound to move on, so we took the train to Nagoya, where we dined, and saw the fine old castle and city, and then by night mail to Yokohama on 9th May.

We found Yokohama full of English travellers, bound for the Chicago Exhibition, and we went to the Club Hotel, which was comfortable and close to the club, also a very good one.

Our friend Colonel Henry Robinson, and many others, were at the Grand Hotel—which was more fashionable—at the other end of the Bund, close to the celebrated curio shops and the creek which divides the Bluff from the town. There were many pleasant houses between, all facing the sea. We found several old friends still located here, and we were hospitably entertained by Mr. and Mrs. Dodds, of Messrs. Butterfield & Swire, a great steamer and business firm in these parts, and by Messrs. Jardine's agent, who also had a charming country house near the racecourse.

There are lovely detached houses on the Bluff and Mississippi Bay.

The *Empress of India*, of the new Vancouver line of steamers, left full of passengers, with many of our friends, on 12th May, and there was a comparative calm in the community of Yokohama. We, of course, visited the great bronze image of Daiboots, or Daibutsu, and the neighbouring town of Kamakura, where there is a capital hotel; but twenty-five years before two English officers stationed at Yokohama had been cut down here and killed by the Samaurai, or two-sworded men, who were wandering about the country after the break-up of the Daimios or feudal princes, when the government of the Mikado was being consolidated. Those were troublous times, and a whole battalion of infantry, with a detachment of artillery and sappers, were quartered in Yokohama to protect the Legation and residents from threatened attacks by the Japanese. In 1870 all the foreign Legations had armed escorts. The barracks on the Bluff have been converted into residential houses, and the hospital was occupied by a friend of mine, who had made it quite a nice place.

There are many pretty walks, drives, rides, and "rickshaw" roads all over this part, which is hilly, with lovely views of the sea, and we saw the Japanese fleet performing here. The rickshaw, or "ginrickisha"—which is, I believe, the correct way of spelling it—was introduced into Japan about twenty years ago. I can remember when only cangos or norimonos (native palanquins) were the carriage of the country; but now these stout little Japs run along about twenty-five miles a day, with very little refreshment, at a cost of 75 cents—say 3s. each man. I usually had two, and sometimes three, at hills, as they said I was too heavy for one coolie.

We paid a visit to the dockyard at Yokosuka, where the Government build cruisers and gun-boats, and it is practically the headquarters of their navy. The ships were nearly all out at manœuvres, under Captain Ingles, R.N., when we got there, but the flag-lieutenant, a very nice Jap, showed us over the place, and gave us an excellent lunch, beginning with beer and ending with champagne, and told me that they could make everything we saw there except the machines themselves, and very soon they expected to do that. I dare say they do now, for they can copy anything.

The principal sight here is the grave of William Adams, who about the year 1600 was made a prisoner by the Japanese, after being a chief pilot in the Dutch service, and was employed as a ship-builder and agent, and lived for twenty years at Yokosuka, where he was much respected. It will be interesting to R.E.'s to know that he came from Gillingham, Kent. He was the first Englishman that ever resided in Japan. The bay is very pretty and the town picturesque. Nearly all these places are reached by railway from Yokohama, which with its official suburb of Kanagawa, occupies a considerable space. The public buildings are fine, and the Japanese officials transact nearly all their business of the foreign settlement in Kanagawa.

We left by rail on the 15th May for Tokyo, about half-an-hour's ride by express train, and put up at the Club Hotel in Tsukiji, belonging to the same company as the hotel in Yokohama; near the sea and forts.

Tokyo is an enormous city very widely spread out, with new buildings in the official part, a grand old castle where the Mikado lives in the centre, the Legations in the open spaces near; the British being in a sort of lovely park with picturesque buildings, where we were most hospitably entertained by Mr. De Bunsen, the Chargé d'Affaires, the Minister being on leave in England. We started for Nikko on the afternoon of May 16th, when it was very wet, and reached our destination about 7 p.m. We stayed at Kanaya's Hotel, very comfortable and near the temples, most picturesquely situated on a brawling river with a red bridge—over which only the Mikado is allowed to pass when visiting the sacred shrines.

There are beautiful avenues of trees approaching the town in nearly every direction. The temples and gardens are lovely, and only spoilt by the photographers' shops, which tempt you to be taken with a temple background, and groups of Japs and "rickshaws" in front. The views in the neighbourhood of distant mountains, waterfalls, woods, &c., are most charming; but we were reluctantly obliged to leave them and return to Tokyo on the 18th May, as we had still much to see there and at Miyanoshita.

We had a great deal of rain about this time, but usually a fine day between, when the weather was simply beautiful. We explored more temples, parks, and bazaars at Tokyo on 19th May, and in the afternoon left for Yokohama, and thence by train, tram, and rickshaws up a very steep road, very much in the rain, to Miyanoshita, the beautiful hill resort of Yokohama society. We arrived at Fuji-ya's Hotel rather late; found it very full; but they packed us away somewhere and we slept peacefully until roused by morning bathers; for the whole of the back of the hotel is one line of baths—hot naturally and cooled artificially.

Then we started with chairs and coolies to see Lake Hakoné and the beautiful hill country near; it was really lovely weather, and we got to our destination in time for an excellent lunch. We boated from Hakoné to the other end of the lake with a fine view of the sacred mountain Fuji-san, or Fusi-yama, nearly all the way, and arrived at a village called Shin-yu, whence you climb to the Sulphur Springs—Oji-go-ku—very high up on the hills, and then by degrees you drop down to Miyanoshita after a long day's walk in time for a most excellent dinner; all being served by waitresses or nésans, who chattered and laughed as if they thoroughly enjoyed it.

The next day, Sunday, was a lovely afternoon, which we employed in prospecting all the pretty places near, and finished up at the bazaar, where all sorts of tempting sticks, curios, and photographs are displayed. There was a lively party of Americans staying here who always dressed for dinner in the height of fashion with buttonholes, &c., sang late into the night, and never seemed to leave the hotel.

On 22nd May we left this beautiful spot in a damp, white mist and rain, and descended to the plains, where we joined the railway near Odawara, a place I remember in 1870 as staying at one night during a sort of typhoon or hurricane which levelled most of the houses, and our coolies only kept our tea-house roof on by sitting on it, and holding it down by ropes.

On 23rd May we employed our time in buying curios and saying good-bye to our friends, looking at the strolling players and marionettes, at which the Japs are very clever. They have a horrid sort of Punch and Judy show also, with murders innumerable.

It is rather curious that the Japanese officials all seem to wear white Berlin gloves; even the porters, signalmen, and shunters on the railway, down to the village postmen, who trot about with bare legs and a sort of tabard coat with official stamps before and behind, straw sandals, and a mushroom hat. There are any number of post offices and pillar letter boxes. The Japanese policemen, armed with a sword, nearly always with Berlin gloves on, are at every railway station and street corner, and certainly manage to preserve order among the chattering coolies.

We engaged our berths on board the s.s. *Belgic*—formerly a White Star American liner, which came in on 24th May—for Hong Kong, paying about 180 dollars or yen, which at the then rate of exchange would be £24, for the six days' trip. She was a first-rate steamer, with scarcely any passengers, but had an excellent English captain, who was most kind to us.

We finished up our stay at Yokohama—on the Queen's birthday—by attending a big cricket match, at which the playing was rather wild. We drank the Queen's health at our friends the Dodds' house, at lunch, and went on board the *Belgic* to dine and sleep, being just inside the breakwater recently constructed by the late General Palmer, R.E., who also had carried out the water supply at Tokyo and other important works for the Japanese.

One of the English celebrities in Japan is a Captain Brinckley, late of the Royal Artillery, who was originally artillery instructor to the Japanese army, and now owns the best newspaper published in Tokyo, and is an important factor in the political world. He was the officer commanding a detachment of Royal Artillery in Yokohama when I was there in 1870. He is undoubtedly a very clever man, and the safest authority on curios. The best modern books on Japan we saw were *Murray's Guide*, very good, and Norman's *New Japan*, very interesting. There are, of course, many others. We calculated that our expenses in Japan for four weeks, including travelling, were about £100, which is not, I consider, unreasonable.

We were only sorry that our time was too short to travel further into this beautiful country, which can now be so easily explored by "road, river, and rail."

VI.

We left Yokohama very early, about daylight, and dropped down the lovely Yeddo Bay before breakfast, on 25th May, 1893. We had the steamer *Belgic* almost entirely to ourselves. There were, I think, two American passengers going to China, besides the captain and officers, in the saloon. The steamer was beautifully fitted up, and we quite revelled in plenty of space. No doubt she carried Chinese passengers, but we saw little or nothing of them, their accommodation being quite separate. In former days the Pacific Company's house-on-deck side-wheel walking-beam steamers used to carry as many as 1,200 Chinese, and had to take elaborate precautions to prevent a rising or riot among them by having steam and water pipes and hose ready to play on the offending parties. The steamers from California also used to carry back to China the remains of the Chinese who had died when making the Pacific Railway, &c., to be buried in the graves of their ancestors.

It does seem rather hard on "John Chinaman" that, having been used by the Americans to make their railways and improve their country, particularly in California, he should now be ousted, as he interferes with their labour market, and a heavy tax is placed upon his head, and every effort made to prevent him landing at all.

The Chinamen do get in somehow both in America and Australia, the attempts at photographing them for identity when claiming naturalisation as citizens being, I certainly should say, a failure—as most Chinamen are very like each other, at all events in particular districts—and a roaring trade is, I believe, done in California with these photographs.

We passed several volcanoes off the coast of Japan, but they never seemed to smoke when you wanted to see them I have seen them at night very active, but not during this voyage. We passed near the Loo-Choo Islands on the 27th-28th May, and on 29th were well through the Formosa Straits or channel, sighting the high lands in China near Foo-Choo, Amoy, and Swatow. I see our longest run was three hundred and twenty-four miles, but we averaged about thirteen knots without any pressing. On 30th we sighted the mountains near Hong Kong, and about 2 p.m. went in through the picturesque Lye-e-moon Pass—just meeting the *China*, a corresponding steamer, going to Yokohama and San Francisco, but unable to communicate, which was a "sell" for our captain and officers, who wanted to send letters.

We said farewell to our courteous captain, and landed at the Hong Kong Hotel, which was as hot in late May as it was cold in early March, and the mosquitoes and other inconveniences had begun in earnest; so we took ourselves the next afternoon to the Mount Austin Hotel at the Peak, where we remained three days before our steamer went to Australia. The Peak was lovely in the daytime, but rather misty, damp and cold in the night and early morning; however, you could sleep comfortably.

Nearly all Hong Kong society was living at the Peak in the hotels and pretty houses near ; there were lawn tennis parties, dinners, and other amusements going on. We were hospitably entertained by Colonel Mulloy, the C.R.E., and others, until we had to pack again for our three weeks' voyage on 3rd June.

We had fortunately secured our berths on board the *Chang-sha*, belonging to the China Merchants' Company; it was quite full. Major Bennet and Lieutenant Lloyd, R.E., were going down to Australia on leave, and many other pleasant passengers, among them our doctor, who had been recently saved from the wreck of the *Bokhara;* he was quite the life and soul of the party, and sang very well. We said farewell to our numerous friends, had lunch with the hospitable manager of the Hong Kong and Shanghai Bank, a great factor in China business, and went on board the *Chang-sha*, leaving again by the Lye-e-moon Pass about 4 p.m. on 3rd June. Just in front of us was H.M.S. *Mercury*, going down to the Pescadores to erect a monument to those who had been lost in the wreck of the *Bokhara*. Amongst them was the cricket team returning from Shanghai to Hong Kong. A most liberal subscription was raised among the residents to help the widows and orphans of several officers and soldiers lost in the team besides others ; and the well-known generosity of China society was shown admirably in this instance.

Our Captain Williams in the *Chang-sha* was a capital skipper ; he always made himself most agreeable to the passengers, and in a voyage of three weeks it is a great boon not to be interfered with by vexatious rules. It was getting very hot at first, and most of the men and passengers slept on deck, or in the pretty saloon which was athwart-ships near the centre of the steamer. The cabins were small but comfortable, and we had good bath-rooms. We paid 190 dols.—or about £25—each for our passages; but a very good table was kept, and although we were crowded in the cabins, there was plenty of room in the saloon and on deck.

On 5th June we were off Manila, in the Philippine Islands, sighting the lighthouse, &c., at the entrance to the bay, and after this day, until we made Port Darwin on the North Coast of Australia, we were hardly ever out of sight of land—in fact, it was perfect yachting. The weather was fine, we had some wind and rain, and a bad thunder storm, but nothing to complain of. We were much interested in the picturesque old Spanish and Dutch ports and islands we sighted daily. We passed through the Sooloo Islands, and then made for the Moluccas, passing close to the north-east end of Celebes, then by the Booroo Straits and Amboyna to the east point of Timor, and through the Arafura Sea to Port Darwin, which we reached on 12th June. It is situated well inside Bathurst and the Melvile Islands in Clarence Strait, and the actual town is called Palmerston.

There is an overland telegraph from this place to Adelaide, in South Australia, under which colony it is governed, so we promptly sent a wire to our Western Australian friends, *via* Adelaide, to tell them of our arrival on their continent again. There is also a railway from Port Darwin to some mines, I think about 150 miles off, but there is only a train every other day.

We walked about the town, being much amused by a Parliamentary Election which was going on. I forget the number of electors in this northern district, but it seemed rather small to return a member who would sit about 1,500 miles away, and take three weeks to get there. The general idea is that sooner or later the Northern District, including Northern Queensland, will have to be made into a separate colony.

Port Darwin has the reputation of being the hottest and most malarious place in Australia, but as we were there in the winter, having crossed the Equator on 9th June near Tirnato, in the Molucca Sea, we did not find the temperature unpleasant.

We left on the afternoon of 12th June through Dundas Strait and by Port Essington (once a military station) to the North Coast, and then across the broad Gulf of Carpentaria to Torres Straits, and thence to Thursday Island, which we approached without a pilot, as he did not come off, although signalled for. We reached this imperial coaling-station soon after breakfast on 15th June, having passed a wreck of a large sailing ship, with all masts and rigging standing, looking at a distance as if in full sail; she was full of coal, and went on a reef hard and fast some months before. It is very cramped and difficult navigation about here, and a large steamer of the Queensland and Singapore Mail Line had been wrecked not long ago and many lives lost. We saw one of the survivors at Thursday Island, who had been saved by the merest accident.

It is, however, a great advantage to the Colony of Queensland having this duplicate line of steamers to Europe, as passengers can go by P. and O. or Orient *viâ* Sydney, or by this northern route, according to dates and seasons.

I may mention here that General Sir Henry Norman, the

Governor, whom we met in Sydney, had been all over this Northern District wherever he could possibly travel, and, for a man of his years, was wonderfully active and energetic.

Thursday Island has now become a very important place, as it is the N.E. coaling station of Australia, fortified and protected by S.M. mines. The other coaling station, at Albany, King George's Sound, Western Australia, at the S.W. corner of Australia, is similarly protected.

Some of our party visited the barracks, just completed, and described the arrangements as very perfect. The garrison of fifty men from the Queensland Artillery Defence Force, with, I think, two officers, one of whom had qualified at Shoebury, arrived the day after we left, 15th June, 1893.

I imagine it is intended to relieve this force every two years, for the isolation would be rather trying. Thursday Island is very picturesque, tropical, and, although hot, I believe fairly healthy. Many steamers call, and there is a mixed population of Australians, Malays, Japanese, and other people employed in pearl fisheries and similar pursuits. They were ruled by a Mr. Douglas, a very experienced official, with a police force capable of acting on land or sea. There are some very amusing stories related about this remote region; but things have now settled down into a regular colonial life under the Government of Queensland, which extends over nearly a quarter of the continent of Australia. Brisbane, however, is 1,200 miles off, and sooner or later a separate northern colony must be established.

I see by my notes that the s.s. *Chang-sha* averaged about 280 knots a day since we left Hong Kong, but allowing for currents, &c., I expect she was a twelve-knot steamer at best.

After leaving Thursday Island, which is on the north of

the Endeavour Strait, so named by Captain Cook after his ship, you pass close to Cape York and Albany Island, so that you could almost "throw a biscuit" or anything else on shore; but the channel is properly buoyed and lighted, and our good skipper seemed to know his way about, if I might use the simile, "like an experienced 'bus-driver in London," constantly going up and down through or inside the Great Barrier Reef, which we were now approaching; he was always on the look-out, and after entering the Barrier Reef you are supposed to anchor at night, or when it is dark. There are lighthouses and beacons which you "pick up" in threading your way through this 700 or 800 miles of protected waterway. So much has been written about this freak of nature called the Barrier Reef, that I do not propose to enlarge upon the subject; but I understand, except in very bad weather, it is almost always smooth water inside, when you can see the ocean waves breaking on the reefs outside, and you pass many islands and thriving settlements on the mainland which make the voyage most interesting.

On 16th June we stopped off Claremont Island to give newspapers, letters, and communicate with the lightship, and on 17th we reached Cook Town, but too far off to land comfortably, a steam launch only coming out to take cargo, &c. There is a telegraph from this place to Thursday Island and to the south, which we made use of to communicate with our friends. On 18th June we anchored off Townsville, but being Sunday, it was a long time before any steamer came from shore, so that we had not time to land after medical and Customs examination; but some of our passengers visited the lighthouse near Magnetical Island to get fish, &c. From Townsville there is a railway into the interior to the celebrated Charters Towers Goldfields, and other places. Townsville is a very important place, with a capital bay and anchorage, and the neighbourhood of the Burdekin River is, I believe, very well settled. We passed Northumberland Island on 19th June, very picturesque, and on 20th went through the Great Sandy Strait, which was very pretty and well lit.

On 21st we entered Moreton Bay very early, and steamed up to the lightship off the Brisbane River. We could not go up to Brisbane, as there had been recent floods, which altered the course of the river and displaced the buoys, &c. Much damage was done to the lower parts of the city, and a railway bridge connecting it with the south and Sydney had been carried away.

We said good-bye to one lady passenger here, who went off in a steam launch to Brisbane; she had been a great traveller in many parts of the world, and was very amusing.

After leaving Brisbane by the north end of Moreton Bay again, we ran down the coast, sighting capes and headlands, passing Port Macquarie and Newcastle, until at 3 a.m. we made the magnificent Southead Electric Light of Sydney at the entrance to Port Jackson on 23rd June, 1893. We had to be inspected critically by Medical Quarantine and Customs officers, for they are very particular here on account of measles, smallpox, &c.; but after a brief detention off the Quarantine Station inside the North Head, where they have a really fine lot of buildings (and where they detained the passengers of the steamer which followed ours from China for about a fortnight), we landed at Miller's Wharf—sorry, I think, to leave Captain Williams and his comfortable steamer, on which we had spent a most agreeable three weeks. We presented our skipper with a suitable testimonial, and we all said good-bye, hoping to meet him and his officers again. One misfortune which had overtaken some of our passengers was accentuated when we arrived at Sydney, as the Australian banks had begun to fail when we were in Japan. Many people were obliged to return in a hurry, some were left almost penniless, unable to get out their deposits, and at every telegraph station we came to on the coast anxious enquiries were made about what banks had failed since the last news. I was very thankful to say that the bank where money for my Australian tour was awaiting me remained open.

We took ourselves off to the Australian Hotel in Castlereagh Street, which we made our home for the time we were in Sydney, and a more comfortable or better managed hotel does not exist in Australia. It is looked after by an American and his wife, who thoroughly understand their business, has a capital restaurant, and is not expensive considering the comfort you obtain. It is also the great house of call for visitors, theatre parties, and banquets, and it is central for all amusements.

I had not been in Sydney since 1861, and these thirty-two years had made a vast difference in the appearance of the Capital of New South Wales. Large public buildings had been erected, notably the Post Office, Town Hall, and Public Offices, many new clubs and theatres built, and the suburbs, of which there are many, had extended enormously. I should say that the population had more than doubled, and all the available spots on the north shore and pretty bays around Port Jackson were covered with houses where hardly any existed at my first visit. We paid our respects to the Governor, the late Sir Robert Duff, and his charming family, to General Hutton (of Mounted Infantry fame), commanding the forces, to the Chief Justice, Sir Fred. Darley, and his wife (the sister of our Lady Scratchley), and we were looked after by Renny-Tailyour, R.E., and others, among them my old friend and contemporary Colonel F. C. Roberts, late R.A., and now Military Secretary for Defences. The Admiral Bowden-Smith, his wife and family, also were very kind to us at their pretty house, which used to be called " Kirribilli Point," on the north shore. We attended service at the cathedral, were present at a big reception at Government House on the occasion of the Duke of York's wedding in London, visited the theatres, and were entertained at a great function at the Mint, where the new gold coinage was stamped before issue by Lady Duff. We paid a visit to Kiama, and other places down south near Illawarra, and after four weeks' pleasant stay in Sydney, except for the cold and wet, which were too much for enjoyment, we decided to take ship and go to New Caledonia, the New Hebrides, and Fiji, in the s.s. *Rockton*, on 20th July, to get a little warmth into our systems.

I almost forgot to mention that on 8th July we attended the first review by the Governor and General Hutton of the Defence Force of New South Wales, which was most successful and witnessed by thousands. The R.E. shone out well, the Permanent Artillery are very fine men, and the Lancers and Mounted Infantry came in for great applause, their horses and equipment being very workmanlike. The new organisation was considered most satisfactory, and their medical and ambulance arrangements were very good.

I had the opportunity given me by Dr. Vandeleur Kelly, of the Order of St. John of Jerusalem, to which we belong, of seeing the details of their system, and we were present when Sir Robert Duff, the Governor, presented medals and certificates to successful candidates at the St. John's Ambulance examination, which had taken place just about the time of our arrival in Sydney. They are very keen about this matter, and their defences generally, subjects on which I shall have something more to say in a later paper.

VII.

WE went on board the s.s. *Rockton* in the evening of 20th July, at one of the numerous wharves near Dawes Point in Sydney Harbour.

The steamer was loading until late at night, as we had to take on board forty mules, twenty old horses, and a great deal of cargo for New Caledonia and Fiji. We had also several families on board, and a Fijian nurse called "Anna," who was very ill the greater part of the time.

We cleared the "Heads" about midnight, the harbour, being beautifully lighted, principally by electricity.

The cabins were rather full, at all events as far as Nouméa, in New Caledonia, but we were comfortable enough for a trading steamer, and the saloon was large and airy.

Our Captain Calder was most kind and attentive, and did everything he could to make our voyage pleasant.

It was a little rough at first, for we were soon out of sight of the land of New South Wales, on 21st July, as we shaped our course about N.E. for New Caledonia.

We had quantities of vegetables on board for the French settlement, where apparently they could not produce them, and really there was but little room to move about on deck except with a struggle. The horses and mules had a knack of biting at you when you passed them, and they kicked and squealed very much at night.

Some of the lady passengers suffered a good deal, as we rolled occasionally, although the weather was fine after the first day. There was one very amusing Scotch-American on board, who had been through the War of Secession, and was now going to Nouméa as an agent for some nickel mines worked by a syndicate in Sydney. There is a large production of this metal in New Caledonia.

On 25th July we made the lighthouse on Amédée Island, took a pilot on board, and went in through the Bulair Passage to Nouméa about 5 p.m. It is rather difficult navigation, as there are many rocks, shoals, and small islands near the Passage.

We made fast to the wharf near the market-place, but the French authorities are rather particular, because there are always a large number of convicts at work in or near the harbour, and they are "interned" at night on a small island, or peninsula, where the prison is situated. They seemed to us very harmless, but occasionally I believe give a great deal of trouble.

The town itself is rather picturesque, there are many wooded hills about, and some very pretty drives into the country.

The Convict Band, or "Musique de la Transportation," quite a large one, dressed in suits of loose white flannel and straw hats, play twice a week at night in the Place Nationale, where quite a large audience assembles. They perform remarkably well; their bandmaster was stated to be a murderer, and their discipline is very strict; if they misbehave and play badly they are deported to the prison island.

On 26th our captain, doctor, one of the passengers, and ourselves made up a party to drive to La Coulée, a pretty restaurant in the country, about ten miles off, much affected by bridal parties and others. It took us, I think, about two hours, and there was a wedding party also there—the ceremony having taken place in Nouméa about 8 a.m. We heard their speeches and songs in one of the arbours in the restaurant garden ; the bride was pretty, but slightly coloured, and the chief speaker was the leading advocate of the place. We had a most excellent lunch, washed down by some liqueur made at a neighbouring monastery, and returned to Nouméa early in the afternoon to see what we could of the place. There is a fine cathedral, built by the " deportés," a small club, and some pretty houses. There had been a gale recently, which had unroofed part of the town.

The Governor was away on leave. We called on his deputy, but he was in deep mourning, and did not receive visitors ; we saw him, however, driving in a very good carriage afterwards. My wife and daughter were taken for a drive by some very pleasant residents along the fashionable promenade on the sea-shore, and saw all the rank, beauty, and fashion disporting themselves in the evening.

The French European mail steamers *viâ* Sydney run here every month, and shortly before our visit General Tulloch, the Commandant, from Melbourne, with a party of friends, had been at Nouméa on the occasion of the Fête Nationale, and had been most hospitably received.

The French convicts do occasionally escape from New

Caledonia to the Coast of Australia, but as they have to run their chance in open boats for about 900 miles, it is a very risky proceeding, and they are usually captured by the Australian authorities and returned to the French settlement.

There was an English man-of-war in the harbour, H.M.S. *Tauranga*, which is one of the Australian squadron officered and manned by us and under our Admiral.

The Australian defence squadron, with its headquarters in Sydney, consists of five ships—four in commission and one in reserve—besides two torpedo catchers paid for by the Colonies; there are other men-of-war on the station. The French and English men-of-war at Nouméa take it in turns to visit the adjacent New Hebrides Islands, over which we exercise a sort of joint protectorate.

We went on board the *Tauranga* to tea, and were shown over the ship by the captain and officers, for whom we had brought a domestic cat from friends in Sydney.

Early in the morning of 27th July we left for Vila, a port in the New Hebrides, going out through the narrow Havannah passage near the Isle of Pines; rather difficult navigation, but very pretty and picturesque.

It was beautiful weather, with a few showers, and after sighting land, on 28th July, we arrived at Vila Harbour, on Sandwich Island, a pretty land-locked bay, about 3.30 p.m. We landed for a walk after tea, but it was too hot for enjoyment.

Vila is a port where a great deal of copra, or dried cocoa-nut, is collected for shipment to Australia and England. The copra is eventually pressed to make oil, and the refuse is used for other purposes.

We had great difficulty in getting our copra shipped; there were no natives handy, and a rival steamship company had endeavoured, I believe, to prevent our steamer taking the cargo. However, by working well over Saturday night, we succeeded in getting our copra shipped from many small boats, and early on Sunday morning, 30th July, we left Vila Harbour for Fiji. Many of the natives in the neighbouring islands are stated to be cannibals. There was an enterprising American who had a phonograph on board, which he was taking round the islands for exhibition; and we had much amusement from its production of some really good music, including that of the " Transportation " band at Nouméa. Some of the natives, including "Anna," were startled by the sounds.

I see by our diary that it was rather rough and windy on 30th and 31st July, and on 1st August we made the lighthouse on Mount Washington, about 8 p.m., fifty miles from Suva in Fiji, and went into the harbour at daylight next morning. We averaged about ten knots during our voyage in the "*Rockton,*" which, considering her appearance, was, I think, pretty fair. She could "rock" a great deal at times. The coast of the large island of Viti Levu, on the south side of which Suva is situated, is very beautiful, and the island of Kandavu, which you pass on the south of the passage, is most picturesque. The vegetation is grand, and the sea very transparent, with constant changes of colour.

We had a pleasant walk on shore on the morning of 2nd of August exploring the town and shops; and in the afternoon drove up into the hills and visited the Chief Justice and other officials.

The Governor, Sir John Thurston, was away at the

Solomon Islands in a man-of-war—I think the *Royalist*, or *Rapid*—his duties as High Commissioner taking him on tours of inspection and inquiry periodically.

We, however, saw his pretty house and garden near the seashore. We dined with Mr. and Mrs. Brown, Mr. Brown being the leading merchant at Suva, at their charming house just beyond the Governor's, and spent a very pleasant evening, being waited on by Solomon Island boys. As far as I could make out, nearly all the work in Fiji is done by imported labour from the Solomon Islands and other places, the native Fijians doing little or nothing, except on their own plantations, being so carefully protected by the English laws and regulations. The Fijians walk well, and the men strut about the place with a splendid carriage. They are not very dark-coloured. The Samoans are also a fine race, less coloured, and walk magnificently. The other islanders are not so upright, but physically fine. The men usually try to lighten the colour of their hair by putting lime on it, which has a very peculiar effect.

There were some prisoners working on the pier who lived in a little house belonging, I think, to the Harbour Master. They seemed to look after themselves, and although locked up at dark, never attempted to escape, being well fed and cared for, and at night they sang psalms until they went to sleep. They formed a crew for the Harbour Master's boat also. There was a very good collection of Fijian and South Sea Island curios at the hotel, and a nice little club, which we inspected.

The Government Offices on the hill at the back of the town are good, and there is a statue of King Thakumbau in the courtyard. He was the last independent chief or sovereign of Fiji, and, I believe, handed over the islands to us in 1874.

The climate of Fiji was cool and pleasant when we were there. There is a great deal of rain at times, and in their summer it must be quite hot enough. I see it stated to be about 90°. These islands are also subject to hurricanes.

On 3rd August we left Suva just after midnight, and reached Levuka, the old capital, on the island of Ovalau, about 6 a.m.; landed mails and some passengers, and left again at 7 a.m. for Labassa, on the north side of Vanua Levu Island, where our horses and mules had to be disembarked for a large sugar estate near Mali Harbour.

As there was no one to meet the steamer when we arrived about 6 p.m., the captain and doctor proceeded up the river in a boat—taking nearly the whole night—to the estate, whence they had to bring down people to land our quadrupeds the next morning. This was really an amusing proceeding, for there were considerable difficulties in getting the mules into slings to put them into flats and boats. They occasionally escaped, and had to be "chivied" all over the deck. However, we at last succeeded in discharging our cargo, and after a long talk with the Labassa estate people, we got under way at 1.30 p.m., 4th August, for Levuka again. It was very beautiful, steaming in and out of these passages and islands, usually inside a reef, somewhat like the Great Barrier Reef on a small scale, with exquisite scenery, and the sea below of a lovely colour and quite clear. We had a little wind at times, and some showers, but the bright fine atmosphere made us wish to live in it altogether.

We anchored for the night near a coral island, as we could not get through some of the passages in the dark;

but left again at daylight on 5th August for Levuka, which we reached at 2 p.m. I may mention that, with the exception of this port and Suva, and near the island of Kandavu, there are no lighthouses, so that a "skipper" has to pick his way as best he can, which makes steamer travelling in this region somewhat exciting ; but I must say that the navigators are most careful, and wrecks or losses are rare.

There is a line of steamers which runs up from Auckland, in New Zealand, every month, and we met one of these in our travels; also a steamer from Melbourne. A French man-of-war, on its way to Tahiti, came into Levuka while we were there, but apparently only to take a Roman Catholic Bishop to see some of his flock on the neighbouring islands.

We landed and walked about the former capital of Fiji with Mr. Garrick, a well-known resident, brother of the Agent-General for Queensland ; called on several officials, and saw as much as we could in the afternoon. The place is pretty, but somewhat decayed. There was, however, cricket going on. The old Government House, built by Sir Arthur Gordon, seemed rather dilapidated. I fancy the greater part of the trade and business has gone to Suva, which is on quite a large island—Viti Levu—while Levuka is situated on the small island of Ovalau on the east of Suva, in rather a contracted position. The large island of Vanua Levu, on which is Labassa, lies to the north of Suva and Levuka, and has several smaller islands round it, which look very picturesque.

As far as I understand, the colony is governed on the principle of there being a small number of European commissioners and stipendiary magistrates, and a large number of native chiefs, called Roko-Tuis and Bulis, in the provinces, which have their councils and look after the taxes, &c., under the supervision of the Legislative Council of the Colony. The system apparently works well and cheaply. The Rokos and Bulis we saw walked about with an official stick or staff, which they were very proud of.

There are a considerable number of sugar estates on the islands. The one at Labassa, for which we took the mules and horses, and another on the Rewa River, near Suva, belong to a Sydney company, which I heard was doing very well. There was always the usual difficulty of the labour question, as other coolies have to be imported under rather stringent regulations. This also affects the sugar industry of Queensland, where labour is brought from the South Sea Islands.

Early on 6th August we left Levuka again for Suva, arriving about 2 p.m. As we had been detained so long at Mali Harbour, we were obliged, although it was Sunday, to go down to Navua, a small port inside the island of Mbenga, thirty miles south, to load with bananas for the Sydney market, as every day was of consequence.

We had a good deal of trouble with the owners and people in charge of boats working at night, and it ended in a "few rounds" between an officer of the ship and an agent, in which the latter got the worst of it.

We left Navua the next morning early for Suva, where we took in more bananas and several passengers, amongst them the Attorney-General of Fiji and his family, going to Sydney, with whom we became very friendly. A fine old soldier who had been in Australia and New Zealand for years, and afterwards in the constabulary here, came to interview me about his pension, he having finished his career by being gaoler at Suva, after being sergeant-major and local officer of police. I wrote a letter for him to the Colonial Office ; but I am sorry to hear that he has since died.

We said good-bye to the various people at Suva who had been kind to us ; several of them brought flowers, oranges, and more bananas, and it was like a flower and fruit garden on the poop for some days afterwards.

We were very sorry that we were unable to go up the Rewa River, in Viti Levu, to the estate owned by the colonial sugar company already referred to. We had brought introductions and made arrangements with the manager, but unfortunately our steamer was so late in returning from Levuka that we had not time to stay in Suva for more than a few hours, and it would have taken us nearly two days to do the trip comfortably in a steam launch from Suva.

We left Suva about 2 p.m., 7th August, after our six days in Fiji, delighted with the beautiful country and the lovely transparent sea ; and I cannot imagine a nicer place to spend a holiday if one was in that part of the world again.

We had rather fine weather with slight squalls. Passed Hunter's Island about 8 a.m. on the 9th August, and kept up our usual ten knots until 11th August, when we had a storm, rain and squalls, and rolled heavily. We had a wave over the poop in the afternoon, which upset a good many people, and caused our ladies to withdraw rapidly.

After this the weather improved, and on the 12th (Sunday) it was calm again, but much colder.

On this trip you pass comparatively near Norfolk Island, once a convict station, now peopled by the old Pitcairn Islanders, who were the descendants of the mutineers of the *Bounty*. They were moved there in 1856, but I believe some of them returned to their old island, which is under British protection. Lord Howe's Island, still nearer New South Wales, has a small population, but a delightful climate. Occasionally a shipwrecked crew takes refuge in these islands, and it is difficult to get to them, there being no regular steamer here, and often people are unable to land on account of the surf. The Government sent a steamer while we were away in Fiji, so that we missed the only opportunity we were likely to have. I believe both islands are beautiful. There was on board our steamer a newspaper man, who had lately been in the French island of Tahiti. He was quite enthusiastic about the lovely scenery, which really made us long to go there; but it is difficult to get at, there being no regular communication.

On 14th August we arrived off Sydney Heads about 12 noon, passing the homeward-bound *Orient* mail steamer just outside, and after the usual searching examination by doctors, Customs, etc., we went up the harbour, landed at the company's wharf, and proceeded again to the Australian Hotel saying farewell to our courteous captain and pleasant fellow-passengers, with whom we had been associated for twenty-five days.

I find that we paid for our three passages £54, which was not at all unreasonable, considering what we saw, and the distance travelled.

VIII.

AFTER our return to Sydney on 14th August, 1893, the weather was warmer than when we left; but still cold at times, with some rain and fogs.

We paid a visit to the Hawkesbury River and Gosford to see the fine railway bridges, returning by Hornsby and North Shore line. We went for a Saturday to Monday outing up to Katoomba, in the Blue Mountains, by rail, then on to Mount Victoria and Govetts' Leap, saw the Leura Falls and the really beautiful mountain scenery near inspected the zig-zag railway down the other side of the Blue Mountains to Bathurst, and returned to Sydney on 21st August delighted with our trip into the mountains. This cost us about £10.

We paid several visits by steamer to Paramatta, the North Shore, Manley Beach, St. Leonards, and drove to the South Head to see the lighthouse, batteries, &c. We went by every tramway we could find (mostly steam) to the suburbs and pretty places near—one takes you to Botany Bay, now a pleasure garden on a large scale, with every sort of amusement to spend a happy day in summer. We accompanied Colonel Renny-Tailyour, Commanding Royal Engineer, to see the torpedo stations and forts, the harbour, being well defended; in fact, I believe it is now admitted that there are too many guns. We went the round of our numerous friends to say good-bye, and among them the Admiral, who had returned lately in the *Orlando* from a cruise, and the squadron was gradually concentrating for manœuvres, which took place later on, when the "men-of-war" went down to Hobart, in Tasmania.

We mounted the clock tower at the post-office to get a last grand view of Sydney and its neighbourhood, and on 28th August we went on board the Orient mail steamer *Ormuz* for passage to Melbourne and Adelaide.

We adopted this line instead of going overland, as there is a break of gauge at or near Albury, on the Murray River, between the Colonies of New South Wales and Victoria, where we were told you were turned out in the middle of the night for Customs examinations and change of carriages—anything but pleasant in the winter. This transit takes about twenty hours.

During our stay in Sydney I was made a member of the "Union," Australian, New South Wales, Athenæum, and Warrigal (the squatters) Clubs. They were all good. Some had bed-rooms where a bachelor could put up, and the members were all kind and hospitable.

I think that Mr. and Mrs. Moore, of the Australian Hotel, were most excellent managers, and we were quite sorry to part, after staying six weeks under their care. Our expenses here averaged about £1 a day each.

I have been in a good many parts of the world, but I know of no place out of England, or, perhaps, Europe, where I would rather live than Sydney.

Of course, it is very hot in summer, but you have the Blue

Mountains in the west, and other places south, to fall back on, where it is cool. You can have constant change and amusement, the beautiful harbour is ever present, and you get English news daily and English fashions a month old.

We left Sydney exactly at noon on 28th August, had fair weather all that day and the 29th—coasting round the south-east corner of Australia—and early on the 30th went through the Port Phillip Heads, called Point Lonsdale and Point Nepean, reaching Melbourne, at the other end of Hobson's Bay, about 9 a.m.

This magnificent natural harbour requires somewhat careful navigation, but it is well buoyed and lighted. The *Ormuz* was a sort of floating palace, very comfortable, beautifully decorated, with a charming music saloon, and had most capable musicians amongst the officers, and we were ruled by Captain White, a most courteous and accomplished gentleman, well known on the Orient Line. Nothing could exceed his kindness to us on board.

We stayed from Wednesday, 30th August, to Saturday, 2nd September, alongside the pier at Port Melbourne, taking in cargo, &c. We went up to the city every day by rail or tram in about half-an-hour to call on friends, shop, pay our respects at Government House, visit the Melbourne Club, and see the numerous public buildings, picture galleries, &c.

I found about four old friends, whom I had known in 1861, still living in Melbourne.

On Saturday, 2nd September, at 12 noon exactly, we left the pier for Adelaide, a great crowd being present to see the *Ormuz* off.

The French mail steamer had left on 31st August, and a P. & O. steamer, the *Valetta*, left for Sydney on 1st September, so there is always a great deal of shipping business going on here, besides the smaller steamers which make use of the wharves up the Yarra River in Melbourne itself.

We had rather a heavy swell and disagreeable weather directly we got outside of Port Phillip Heads, and it was stormy and cold nearly the whole way to Adelaide, which we reached about 7 a.m. on the 4th September, landing in the rain in a steam tender at the pier in Port Adelaide ; and, reaching the city by train, we went up to the York Hotel about 12 noon, just a week after our departure from Sydney.

I find that we paid about £20 for our passages, including detention in Melbourne.

Adelaide is, I think, a disappointing place after Sydney and Melbourne. It is, of course, much smaller. Some of the public buildings are fine, and the streets broad and well laid out with trees on each side, and there are public gardens, and very pretty houses in the suburbs ; but it was very wet and windy during our visit, and there had been a great deal of influenza and measles, which prevented people going about much. We were most hospitably entertained by the Chief Justice, Hon. Samuel J. Way, who also holds the dormant commission of Lieutenant-Governor, and he has administered the government so often and so well that I believe the South Australians petitioned the Colonial Office that he should be permanently appointed Governor when Lord Kintore went home last year. He is also a most enthusiastic Mason.

We paid our respects to the Governor who was then living in the pretty Government House in the city. In summer, like many other residents, he goes up to the hills about twenty miles off to escape the great heat of the plains.

We made the acquaintance also of one of the oldest families in South Australia, distinguished in the squatting, social, and political world, some of whose relations we had known in England. The Hon. G. C. Hawker, the head of the family, who died recently, had been Speaker and President of the Council, but when we were there represented an Adelaide constituency in the Assembly; his picture adorned the walls of the Council Chamber. His nephew, the late Captain E. Hawker, R.E., was known to many of us as a most rising Engineer officer in the S.M.M. branch.

There was a very good theatrical company playing at Adelaide, whom we had seen at Sydney. The Brough-Boucicault people were most successful in "The Amazons," and plays of that description.

On 8th September we decided to leave Adelaide for Melbourne overland by rail, as we had much to see in the Colony of Victoria. So we entrained at 3.30 p.m., dined at the Murray Bridge Station about 6 p.m., and arrived in Melbourne the following morning about 9 a.m., breakfasting *en route* at Ballarat station about daylight, 7.30 a.m. There is no break of gauge or change of carriages on this line; you take the same "sleeper" right through from Adelaide. Mr. E. Hawker accompanied us, and we had two very nice saloons, costing about £10 for three tickets. We went to Menzies' Hotel, the oldest and best in Melbourne, where we had engaged rooms; but it was very old-fashioned, rather a contrast to the "Australian" at Sydney in regard to its accommodation, although the restaurant and dining arrangements were very good. We paid our respects to the Governor, Lord Hopetoun, a most energetic and popular young nobleman, whose charming wife we were introduced to at a large public ball at the City Hall later on. His private secretary, Captain Wallington, whose family we knew in England, was quite justly appreciated as having a wonderful memory and the most perfect manner attainable. He now occupies the same position with Lord Brassey. We also renewed our acquaintance with General Tulloch, commanding the Victorian forces, whom we had met previously in Sydney; he had re-organised their army and put it on a proper footing, hampered, of course, by the want of sufficient funds, the tendency of all the Australian colonies at this time being to reduce expenditure to the lowest limit. However, he had a very effective artillery and engineer corps, which was what we saw most of. The police, mounted and foot, struck me as being a very fine body of men, both in this and the other Australian colonies. They are a necessity for the proper administration of the government, both in the town and in the country, and, as a rule, I think they are much admired and respected. The Customs arrangements between the various colonies are most annoying. Why British colonies on the same continent should be allowed to have different tariffs and tax each other I fail to see. After spending a few days in Melbourne, being present at the Mayor's Ball in the splendid City Hall, visiting the pretty suburbs of St. Kilda, Brighton, Toorak, and seeing the opera of " I Pagliacci" excellently performed by Williamson's company, with a gorgeous ballet afterwards, we took the train on 15th September to Bendigo, or Sandhurst, lunched at Kyneton Station, and arrived at our destination at 4.30 p.m. We walked about this old digging town, which now contains 30,000 people, with fine streets, public buildings, and gardens, where forty years ago was a collection of huts and tents; we were fairly comfortable at the hotel, and left next morning by train about 11.30 a.m. for Swan Hill, on the Murray River, with the object of going by steamer to Mildura, near the South Australian frontier, to see the irrigation colony established by the Chaffey Brothers, which we had heard and read a great deal about. We embarked on board the steamer *Ellen* about 6 p.m., and left late at night or early the next morning in a north-westerly direction for Mildura, stopping at several places, such as Wainby, near the junction with the Murrumbidgee River, Euston, and arriving at Mildura, near Wentworth, at the junction with the Darling River, about 9 p.m. on 18th September, nearly forty-eight hours' travelling, principally at night, with strong electric search-light in the bows; we took in and discharged cargo, picked up wood for the furnaces, and generally made ourselves useful to the people living on the river. We passed several wool barges, heavily laden, being towed or under steam; for this waterway extends from the low country south of Adelaide to the Australian Alps, in the south-west of New South Wales. The river has about 2,000 miles navigable for steamers of light draught and flat bottomed.

There is another irrigation colony at Renmark, in the South Australian territory, about one and a half days nearer Adelaide, which we might have reached from the latter place, but we could hardly spare the time. In summer I fancy that the river is so low that navigation is impossible, and these colonies have to be reached by coach overland. The back-water of the Murray is used for irrigating the fruit-growing areas, and there are pumping stations and many irrigation canals. I believe that anything can be grown with care, and the most successful estate we saw at Mildura belonged to Lord Ranfurly, and was looked after by Conway-Gordon, a son of an old Indian R E. friend. It is very hot indeed in summer, we heard. There are some good houses, and a large temperance hotel. On the Victorian side of the Murray River prohibition prevails; on the New South Wales side there are no restrictions; hence there are many complications in the local liquor laws.

After spending two days at Mildura, driving over the greater part of the place, inspecting the dried fruits, irrigation arrangements and system of planting, we left about 10 p.m. on our return to Swan Hill, the steamer from Renmark and the lower part of the Murray having arrived that morning. She had brought up a distinguished Mayor from South Australia, who wore a tall chimney-pot hat and frock coat, and both he and his wife were very smart. The river had been very much in flood, and it was very difficult on both our journeys to discover where the banks were situated, for the gum trees stood out in the water, and occasionally we took short cuts. Even the junctions with the Darling and Murrumbidgee rivers were very ill-defined.

We disturbed thousands of parrots and cockatoos, who screeched and flew away at the noise of the steamer. We saw many wild ducks also. It was rather monotonous, but we stopped very often to take in cargo and a few passengers, and load up with wool. We arrived at Swan Hill again about midnight on 22nd, but did not land until the next morning, when we explored the little town, and left for Bendigo at twelve, reaching our hotel again about 7 p.m.

We stayed there over the Sunday, which was very wet, and saw as much as we could of the neighbourhood—Eagle Hawk mines, &c.—by steam tram, and on Monday, 25th September, we returned to Melbourne, which we reached about 4.30 p.m., after ten days' absence. This trip cost about £28. We stayed at Melbourne until 5th October, the Governor and his party and nearly all the fashionable world being away at the Sydney Race Week; but we had many friends to visit and places to see, and Rainsford-Hannay devoted a long day to us, visiting the forts, &c., at Queenscliffe, near the Port Phillip Heads, in the Government steamer, and returning by Geelong Railway late in the evening.

While on this subject I should like to say that, from what I saw and heard, the harbours of Sydney and Melbourne are very well defended by batteries and S.M. mines; the configuration of the bays lends itself to obstruction, and every advantage has been taken to carry this out. Albany, at King George's Sound, which I have not seen since 1861, is, I understand, equally well defended, and Thursday Island I have described before. Adelaide is partially defended, and about Brisbane I know little; but it seems to me that, where possible, the Australian Colonies, including Tasmania and New Zealand, which we saw subsequently, have endeavoured to protect their principal ports and coaling stations, and it only remains to them by a liberal expenditure to keep up their defences and their forces in touch with modern requirements, as a matter of "Fire Insurance," which they should easily be able to afford. Possibly their eyes have been opened lately to what may happen. I understand that the South Australian Force is at a low ebb.

The connection of the Corps of R.E. with Australasia has been very important. Sir George Gipps, an old Peninsular R.E., governed New South Wales in the forties, and Gippsland is called after him. Sir W. Denison ruled over Tasmania and New South Wales in an eminent degree, and made his mark, which still remains. Sir W. Jervois governed South Australia and New Zealand, and did much to improve the defences generally of Australasia. Sir Andrew Clarke made his influence felt as a young officer in New Zealand and Tasmania, then called Van Diemens Land, and it is to him and Charles Pasley that Melbourne owes much of its prosperity and appearance, from the admirable way they managed the Survey and Public Works Department in the fifties. Sir Edward Ward controlled the Mints of Sydney and Melbourne. Colonel Martindale looked after New South Wales Railways. Sir Peter Scratchley defended the ports and helped to exploit New Guinea, where he lost too soon his valuable life. General Frome and Sir Henry Freeling surveyed South Australia. Sir J. B. Edwards, Sir G. S. Clarke, General Schaw, and Colonel Cautley have of late years assisted in the defences.

Sir Edmund Henderson, Sir Edmond Du Cane, Sir William Crossman, and General H. Wray did much for Western Australia, and Sir Harry Ord governed it wisely. Sir A. Clarke, Generals Collinson, the Moulds (father and son), Brooke and Pasley fought many times in New Zealand, and other officers surveyed Fiji, and were continually called upon to help the different Colonial Governments, and I think it will be admitted by all that the R.E. have very fairly, honestly, and economically aided in the advance of Australia.

On 5th October, after saying good-bye to our numerous hospitable friends in the Service, in the banks and society generally, including the Melbourne and Australian Clubs, we embarked on board s.s. *Pateena* for Launceston, Tasmania, at a wharf in the Yarra River, and left about 2.30 p.m. We got fogged at the Heads, and had to anchor nearly all night, but about 3.30 a.m. we got under weigh again, being able to see the lights, and said farewell to Australia on 6th October, 1893.

After leaving Port Phillip Heads, on the 6th October, 1893, we carried the fog with us across Bass Straits. It was very damp, too, and we had a large number of passengers on board the s.s. *Pateena*, but as there was a piano and a music room, the men generally amused themselves with singing choruses and keeping up their spirits, although there was a chance of our being short of food, as we were only victualled for about twenty-four hours, and the voyage actually took forty-two. We had to anchor off the Bell Buoy, which we could only hear in the fog at the mouth of the River Tamar, nearly all the second night, but we managed to see sufficiently at daylight on 7th October to creep up the river to Launceston, which we reached at 9 a.m.

The distance from Wilson's Promontory, the southernmost point of Australia, where there is a fine lighthouse, is only about 120 miles; but I fancy fogs are very usual here in their winter, and we experienced much the same weather afterwards in approaching the coast of New Zealand. The Customs examination at Launceston was very critical and disagreeable. They dislike the Melbourne tariff, I suppose, and try to increase their own revenue by high duties.

We put up at the Brisbane Hotel, which was rather primitive, but comfortable, with fair cooking. In the afternoon we went by train to Deloraine, about fifty miles to the west, to see some of the agricultural country and scenery, which was very pretty. We walked about Deloraine, and got back to Launceston again about 6.45 p.m. I made the acquaintance of Mr. Gunn, the agent of the Commercial Union Insurance Company, with which some of my family are connected, and he laid himself out to show us all the sights of the neighbourhood, and was a most valuable guide, for he was an old resident, and knew all the traditions of Tasmania, and as I had passed some weeks there in 1861, and some days in Launceston with the present Colonel Seddon, R.E., when we attended a celebrated wedding, it was most interesting to me to hear about old friends and see the old places. We drove to Longford, lunched there on Sunday, 8th October, and returned through Perth and very pretty scenery about 5.30 p.m.

We visited the romantic Cataract Gorge, and drove to Corra-Linn Waterfall with Mr. Gunn on 9th October. After saying good-bye to him on afternoon of 10th, we left by railway for Hobart, 120 miles off, which we reached about 8.45 p m. The Brough and Boucicault Theatrical Company arrived at the hotel in Launceston just before we left, on their tour through Australasia. I may mention that there was a nice little club also, of which I was made a member. We were very sorry to leave Launceston. It is a very pretty place, and has great capabilities; but times were bad in Tasmania, as elsewhere in Australasia, but I trust that things have since improved, and people are better off. The railway journey, about six hours, to Hobart, is very picturesque; but on a bridge approaching the capital there had recently been an attempt to throw the train off the line, which made it rather exciting. I understand that a man was afterwards tried for the outrage and acquitted. At Hobart we went to the Orient Hotel, I believe the only good one there, and that also rather old-fashioned compared with our Australian hostelries, but we were fairly comfortable, and there was a good cook and plenty of room. The weather had improved while we were at Launceston, and we had some bright sunny days, quite warm, at Hobart.

We paid our respects to the new Governor, Lord Gormanstown, walked in the lovely Botanical Gardens, visited the Cascades by electric tram, and made the acquaintance of the Chief Justice (and Lieut.-Governor), Sir W. Lambert Dobson, a connection of mine, and his family, who had a charming house on the hill towards Mount Wellington.

On 12th October we went down to the wharf to greet the s.s. *Arawa*, just arriving from England with another connection of ours, Sir Richard Rennie, the late Chief Judge of the Consular Courts in China and Japan, who had come out to Tasmania, and proposed to go on to New Zealand for fishing, &c. We had timed ourselves to reach Hobart to meet him and hear the latest news of our family and friends.

He put up at the Club, a very pleasant residence and meeting-place, close to the Orient Hotel, of which I had also been made a member. He afterwards accompanied Sir Lambert Dobson on circuit, and saw a great deal of the island. We stayed about a fortnight at Hobart, paying visits to the Queen's Battery, at the entrance of the harbour, on the River Derwent; went over to Bellerive, on the opposite side of the harbour; went to New Norfolk by steamer up the Derwent, and visited the salmon ponds beyond in pouring rain. I believe the introduction of salmon into the island is fairly successful. We visited the Newtown College, of which Colonel Cruickshank, R.E., is Principal, and we made the acquaintance of Colonel Warner, the Commandant, who lived at the old barracks where I had stayed in November, 1861.

We attended service at the cathedral—just opposite our hotel—and visited the House of Assembly and Council Chamber, when a debate was proceeding.

We went some considerable distance up Mount Wellington, which towers above the city, but the weather was too twe during the last week of our stay to do much outing. We however, visited an agricultural show.

There was a most efficient Staff-Sergeant-Instructor, R.E., here, with whom we had a long talk, and who seemed to be a factotum of the Commandant and other officials; and the manager of the Government Railways, who occupies the old R.E. office, gave me a great deal of valuable information. The Governor was away at an agricultural meeting at Longford during most of our stay, and we did not see him, but the Government House is a very good one, and stands beautifully, near the Botanical Gardens, overlooking the river Derwent, and was, I believe, built by the late Sir William Denison, assisted by Sir Andrew Clarke.

After saying good-bye to all the kind friends we had

met, we put ourselves on board the Union s.s. *Wairarapa*, which arrived from Melbourne on the evening of 23rd October, having already made the acquaintance of Captain MacIntosh and the steamer the previous week, when she came in on her way to Melbourne from New Zealand and Sydney. These steamers make the round trip about once a month, calling at various ports *en route*, which I will describe later on. Our expenses in Tasmania were about £55.

Our impressions of Tasmania were that it is very pretty and picturesque, with a more equable climate than Australia and very diversified scenery—hill and dale, mountain and valley, with English-looking rivers, well wooded—and in the N.W. there are some valuable mines, more particularly the Mount Bischoff tin mine, and others; but being principally a pastoral and agricultural country, it has not progressed to the same extent as its neighbours Australia and New Zealand, and although the colonists are very pleasant, agreeable people, they can hardly be called prosperous at present. In the olden days the Melbourne and Sydney marrying young men came down to Tasmania for their wives; the young ladies were very pretty and fascinating, and, if I may say so, still keep up their reputation for beauty.

There is a large influx of people from the Australian Colonies at the summer season to Hobart and Launceston, to escape the heat, and I believe the place is then very gay, particularly when the Naval squadron is there.

The main roads are good, more especially the Hobart and Launceston Road, made originally by convicts, and kept up for stage coaches, which, in 1861, did the 120 miles in, I think ten hours; at all events, I used these conveyances three times in 1861, twice by day and once by night.

There are scarcely any remains of the old convict days—the houses and prisons at Port Arthur have become hotels and stores. I can remember them in 1861 partially filled with the survivors of the convict system, and the barracks were always occupied by a company of infantry. I think there can be no doubt that in the early days transportation was of great use to these colonies in opening up and developing the country. Cheap labour was provided. Public works were carried on which would have been unprofitable for the free population only to accomplish. Excellent roads and bridges were made, and the Imperial expenditure assisted struggling colonies over many difficulties. It is now the fashion to abuse former transportation, but, I think, without it, hardly any of the Australian colonies would have existed.

In the last number of our "Travels" I mentioned the names of R.E. officers connected with Australasia. I think my poor friend Captain A. A. Jopp and Major-General E. H. Steward, C.M.G., should be added as having advised many Agents-General with regard to the defences of the colonies and the armament of their forts and batteries.

We left Hobart about 8 p.m. on 23rd October, going down the Derwent River and estuary, which are very beautiful when you can see them, and passed Tasman's Peninsula, on which is Port Arthur, joined to the mainland by Eaglehawk Neck, which formed the barrier of the old convict settlement, protected by sentries and watch dogs to prevent prisoners escaping, the detachment of infantry being usually commanded by a newly-married subaltern, who occupied the pretty cottage at Eaglehawk for his honeymoon. These are matters of history now ; but I believe the alleged ill-treatment of convicts, at all events in the last fifty years, described in many sensational novels, to be much exaggerated, for I know that in Western Australia, under the probation system there instituted, it was simply impossible for any officials to use extreme measures without being reported.

On the morning of the 24th October we were well out at sea, after sighting various lighthouses the preceding night, and the weather was warm and bright, and quite calm. We read, wrote, played Khanhoo, and were very comfortable on board the *Wairarapa* ; the old captain was most kind ; his cabin on the bridge was a great place for tea, and his dear little Scotch terrier "Daisy" always ready for a game of play. I will describe our last meeting at Auckland later on.

Before we left Melbourne we took our three tickets through Cook's agent to England *viâ* Tasmania, New Zealand, and California, available for, I think, a year, for which we paid about £75 each. This enabled us to break our journey almost anywhere we liked, and gave us the option of three or four lines of railway across the American continent and an American steamer line to Southampton. It is doubtless the most economical way to travel in these parts. We had a fairly full steamer with some pleasant passengers, a few, like ourselves, travelling round the world. On the 25th and 26th October we had rain and foggy weather, but it was fine and calm before we sighted the lighthouse on Puysegur, the south-west point on the South or middle Island, New Zealand, and early the next morning, 27th October, we crept through the fog in Foveaux Straits, until we made the " Bluff " about 8 a.m., and anchored off the wharf of the port of Invercargill, called Campbell-town. You sight the comparatively small Stewart Island on the southern side of the straits, which is used principally by whalers. The latitude, 47° south, makes it very cold in winter. We arrived in what would be our spring, and the weather generally was warm and pleasant, but we had a good deal of rain.

We went up to Invercargill, the capital of Southland, by railway, and spent a pleasant day shopping, seeing the view from the Water Tower, of which the people are very proud, taking a horse tram into the suburbs, where there were some pretty houses, lunching at the hotel (where we stayed afterwards on another trip) and returned to the " Bluff " to join our steamer, leaving about 4 p.m. for Otago and Dunedin. There is a good deal of business done in the season at Invercargill with wool and produce shipped to Europe. There is a battery to protect the entrance into the " Bluff " harbour, which all ships have to pass. We had a roughish night on 27th October, and we got caught in a fog off the Heads of Otago harbour, and only reached Port Chalmers about 10 a.m., too late for the tide to take us up to Dunedin until 4 p.m.

Port Chalmers, is, however, very pretty and picturesque, and we spent the day very pleasantly, walking about and seeing the pretty views and houses. We purchased a photograph of our old steamer, the *Nairnshire*, which had been to this port since we left her in Western Australia in December, 1892, to load for England with frozen meat, being the principal article of export in this part of New Zealand.

We eventually reached Dunedin about 6 p.m. The harbour is banked and artificially deepened and dredged to enable large steamers to lie alongside the wharves of the city, but it has been carried out at an enormous cost, some people think quite unnecessarily, as Port Chalmers is connected by railway and is a good harbour itself. The configuration of Dunedin is rather peculiar, being only separated from the ocean by a narrow strip of sand hills less than one and a half miles wide, which it has been suggested should be pierced or tunnelled for drainage purposes, the sewage, &c., of the city and neighbourhood being now discharged into the harbour, which should be prejudicial to health, and is often very unpleasant to the nasal organs. However, I believe Dunedin is at present healthy enough, but there are often very strong breezes.

We put up at the Grand Hotel, where we were fairly comfortable; it was noisy at times, but they did their best for us.

We had a good deal of rain and wind also, but these did not interfere with our sight-seeing and visits to the pretty suburbs and houses of many friends who called upon us. Mr. and Mrs. Perston, of the Bank of New South Wales, were very kind and attentive; Mr. Mills, managing director of the Union Company's steamers, and his wife; Judge Williams, of the Supreme Court, and his charming wife and family; Mr. Rattray and his family; and Mr. and Mrs. Larnach were all most hospitable. Dunedin is essentially a Scotch community, and, as my family is of Scotch extraction, nothing could have been more friendly than the attention of the residents to us. There was a very nice club, almost in the country, where I met Colonel Fox, R.A., the active commandant of the New Zealand forces, whom we had known as A.D.C. to General W. H. Goodenough, R.A., in England. He was gradually re-organising the New Zealand army, but met with much opposition at the time; but I believe this has been overcome, and he is now a Secretary for defences of the colony, with a staff of officers under him.

After being a week at Dunedin we decided, on 4th November, to pay a visit to the Cold Lakes, which you reach by train, leaving about 8 a.m., viâ Gore (the junction for Invercargill), as far as Kingston, the terminus on the southern end of the Lake Wakatipu, where you find a steamer which takes you to Queenstown, about the centre of the chain of lakes, where there is a capital hotel, which we reached about 9.30 p.m.; we found the rival candidates for a parliamentary election then going on staying there, and a bride and bridegroom whom we had seen married in the cathedral at Dunedin some days before. We drove about the country near Frankton on Sunday, 5th November, after attending service in a mission chapel.

On Monday, 6th November, we started by steamer again from Queenstown about 10 a.m., and went on to the head of Lake Wakatipu, stopping at Kinloch, and then to Glenorchy, where there is an excellent little hotel, from which excursions are made to Mount Earnslaw, 9,165 feet high, with glaciers and other Alpine excitements. We only looked at it from a respectful distance, although it is periodically ascended. The region more towards the south-west is no distance overland from the West Coast Sounds, which you approach by steamer and are very beautiful. Excursion steamers run in the summer from Dunedin, Invercargill, &c., but we were too early in the season for them. The Government steamer, called *Hinemoa*, in which our friend Sir Richard Rennie obtained a passage, left Wellington about the time we were at the lakes for a cruise on the West Coast, calling at Westport, Greymouth, and Hokitika on the way, and the scenery in these numerous sounds, or fiords, was described to me as most beautiful and romantic. There are other lakes, such as Te-anau, Manipuri, Wanaka, and Hawea, which can be reached by coaching, and which we heard were well worthy of a visit. The mountains on each side of the lake are very fine, the Hector Range and Richardson Mountains particularly so. I see that our three tickets for this trip, including most hotels, cost us £27.

We returned to Queenstown on 7th November, and on the 8th took a long drive to Arrowtown by Arthur's Point mines; in fact, this is all a mining district, which our rival candidates at the hotel wished to represent in the Assembly, and where they addressed political meetings every night. I am sorry to say that our friend was eventually defeated.

On 9th November, in pouring rain, we returned by steamer to Kingston, and then, after a scrambling lunch at the so-called hotel, we took the train to Lumsden, and thence to Invercargill, which we reached about 8.30 p.m., after ten hours' travelling, very hungry and tired. Some of the country was interesting. We had but little time next day to see much more of Invercargill, leaving at 11 a.m., and reaching Dunedin *via* Gore and Clinton (where we lunched) at 7.30 p.m. Part of the line was flooded, and travelling was slow in consequence.

We paid a visit on 17th November to Oamaru, about

eighty miles north of Dunedin by rail, to see some friends. There was an agricultural meeting going on, and the pretty seaport town was very full. We returned the same evening, through very pretty scenery, and many tunnels near Blueskin Bay and Port Chalmers, to Dunedin.

IX.

THE day after we returned from Oamaru, the Governor of New Zealand, the Earl of Glasgow, with the Countess and their suite, left Dunedin by train for Christchurch, after their visit to Melbourne, where they had been present at the races when the Cup was run for, which is a great week in the capital of Victoria. We were introduced to the Viceregal family, and met them again at Christchurch later on in the month. We paid our farewell visits to our numerous friends in the pretty suburbs of Roslyn, St. Clair, and St. Kilda, reaching them by the cable tramways, which help one up the hills.

We also spent a day at Mr. Larnach's splendid Castle, called the Camp, overlooking the sea and the harbour. We drove round the Queen's drive, went to the Museum, to the Botanical Gardens, visited the fine Churches, saw the woollen manufactories, and on the 20th November we packed up our trunks, and put ourselves on board the Union s.s. *Tarawera*, to go up the coast to Port Lyttleton for Christchurch.

We took only a few passengers, and the *Tarawera* was a fairly comfortable steamer; but after leaving Port Chalmers, about 2 p.m., we had a high wind and heavy sea, with a fog which enveloped us before we reached Lyttleton, about

7 a.m. on 21st November; the steamer was very light, and rolled and pitched about a good deal. We landed after breakfast and took the train for Christchurch, which we reached about 10 a.m., and went to Coker's Hotel, celebrated throughout New Zealand as being the best hostelry in the colony, and although it was a rambling sort of wooden building, the rooms were comfortable, and the restaurant portion excellent; we came in for the strawberry season here, and it was a great luxury to us after more than a year's travelling about the world to come across a real English fruit and capital cream. It was very hot, oppressive weather when we arrived, but it turned next day to heavy rain.

Our relative, Sir Richard Rennie, arrived on 22nd November in the s.s. *Flora* from Dunedin, and gave us a most interesting account of his voyage in the *Hinemoa* round the West Coast Sounds, where his party had several exciting adventures at the various sounds or fiords. He left again that evening to join his steamer at Port Lyttleton for Wellington, after driving out with me in a pouring rain in an excellent hansom to call upon the Governor, Lord Glasgow, at a very pretty house, called "Ilam," he had taken for the season.

We called upon several residents to whom we had introductions, and they lived generally in pretty suburban houses with nice gardens; there were horse-trams to most of these places, and also to the seaside resorts, Sumner and New Brighton. We walked about the city, saw the fine Cathedral in the principal square, did a certain amount of shopping, and I was made a member of the capital clubs, the Christchurch and Canterbury, which I found a great convenience.

On Saturday, 25th November, we started for Akaroa on Bank's Peninsula, about forty miles off, at 8.15 a.m. by train to Little River, which is reached about 11 a.m.; then a beautiful coach drive takes you across the hills to Akaroa, passing some old villages which were originally settled by the French, who nearly took possession of this part of the country in 1839-40 ; fortunately, we forestalled them. Akaroa is a very pretty little town, in a most excellent sheltered harbour, where the inhabitants of Christchurch go for Saturday to Monday outings in the hot season. There is plenty of boating, and I think fishing, to be had ; a regatta was to take place soon after we were there, and men-of-war and other steamers occasionally put in to give the people a treat. We stayed at a most comfortable little hotel almost on the water's edge, saw a cricket match, attended a very nice service in the church on Sunday, took a long walk in the romantic hilly neighbourhood afterwards, and returned to Christchurch on Monday afternoon, very much pleased with our excursion. There was an election also pending there, and we heard a great deal about politics generally in New Zealand, for the ladies have votes, and on 28th November at Christchurch the Radicals carried the day, and supported the existing ministry of Mr. Seddon for another term.

There was much enthusiasm when the transparencies at the newspaper offices at night announced to the public the number of votes in the various constituencies, but there was no rioting or rowdyism.

We remained at Christchurch from Monday, 27th November, until Saturday, 2nd December, being present at a charming afternoon party at "Ilam," given by the Governor and Lady Glasgow, on 30th November, at which all the rank, beauty, and fashion of Christchurch were present ; the gardens were very well laid out and pretty, and we thoroughly enjoyed ourselves.

We paid a visit to the fine Museum and beautiful Botanical Garden on the river Avon, and after lunching with Lady Cracroft Wilson, one of the oldest and most respected residents, we went down to Port Lyttleton on the afternoon of 2nd December, and embarked on board the Union s.s. *Rotorua*, for Wellington. We walked about the very interesting town of Lyttleton in the evening, and from the hills at the back, which are pierced by a long railway tunnel, you get magnificent views, and eventually, after waiting for two newly elected ministers, we left the harbour about 10 p.m., very full of passengers.

We had a very rough passage that night, and a great deal of rain the next morning ; but we arrived at Wellington, the capital of New Zealand, about 2 p.m. on Sunday, 3rd December.

Our old friend, General Schaw, R.E., came off to see us, and we walked about the city, making arrangements for our stay after our return in the *Rotorua*, which was going round by Picton and Nelson, in Cook's Straits. We dined and slept on board, and left about noon on Monday, 4th December, for Picton, on the north end of the Middle Island, and south side of Cook's Strait. We arrived there about 6 p.m., the weather being rather rough and wet, but we had a walk on shore in this rather uninteresting town, with a fine view of Queen Charlotte Sound, and left again at 10 p.m. for Nelson. About 4 a.m. on 5th December we got up to see the celebrated " French Pass " between the mainland and the Island of D'Urville. There is a tremendous current always running ; the pass is very narrow, and every precaution is taken to "shoot" it carefully. After going through you are in Tasman's or Blind Bay, and about two nours' more steaming takes you to Nelson, which is well situated, and is a nice little city, with a Cathedral, churches, banks, schools, museum and public institutions of all kinds, and pretty country round it. We got a carriage, and drove about with a very amusing old soldier and ex-policeman, who had been in most of the New Zealand wars, and was quite a magazine of interesting stories of the old times. The country houses were picturesque, and the drive pleasant. We returned to our steamer at lunch, but were prevented by rain from doing much in the afternoon. We left again about 6 p.m., went through the "French Pass" at 9 p.m., and reached Picton about 2 a.m. on 6th December, and returned to Wellington at 8 a.m., after our pleasant two days' excursion in Cook's Straits.

The views of the harbour are most beautiful, and it seemed to us that this part of the world is highly favoured with magnificent scenery, a fine climate, and pleasant occupations. We stayed at the "Occidental" Hotel, where we were only fairly comfortable, but as we intended moving about a good deal, this did not affect us much.

The Wellington Club, where I found General Schaw and Colonel Fox again, was very good, and the few residents we knew were very kind.

There are many tram lines to the suburbs, and locomotion is very easy.

I saw some very good drill by the local forces while staying here, and the forts and batteries protecting the harbour were manned by the artillery during our visit; but I do not think that the service is so popular as in Australia. There were difficulties also with the Ministry, which I believe have since been overcome.

Sir William Jervois, when Governor, of course, helped enormously in the defence of New Zealand.

The public buildings at Wellington are fine, and constructed of wood, and the Government House is pleasantly situated in a large garden with many trees, willows, &c.; the hill rising at the back of the town gives it a picturesque appearance, and the beautiful harbour in front completes a perfect scene.

There was nothing going on in Parliament when we were there, as the elections were hardly completed, and the Governor was staying at Christchurch. We met Sir John Hector, whose acquaintance I had originally made at Hobart, at the Museum, for he is the great geological authority in this part of the world, and we paid a visit to his pretty house at Petone, on the Hutt River. He was a most interesting companion, and his family were very kind and courteous to us. He had just returned from a conference at Adelaide. The Lower Hutt is a very pretty district, with beautiful gardens.

On Saturday, 9th December, we started off by the Manawatu Railway to Palmerston, about 100 miles on the line to New Plymouth in a northerly direction. We left at 1.20 p.m., and arrived at 7.30, a very pleasant six hours' ride. We were very comfortable at the "Occidental" Hotel, and walked about the town, attended a fine church on the Sunday, and in the afternoon drove to Woodville, through the Manawatu Gorge, a most romantic spot, with the river below, and the railway scooped out on one side of the gorge, and the road on the other. I believe there have been several accidents there which added to the excitement. We were fairly comfortable at a small hotel that evening, and next morning we started in the coach at 9.30 a.m. for Eketahuna, through lovely bush scenery, arriving at 1 p.m. ; lunched at the hotel, and took the train over the Rimutaka Mountain, up a steep grade of 1 in 15 with most wonderful engineering appliances. The scenery was most beautiful. The train waits some little time at Masterton, the chief town of the Wairarapa district, and apparently a very thriving place.

We reached Wellington, coming down the valley of the Hutt, about 8 p.m., after a most pleasant excursion ; the weather was fine, and everything was in our favour.

We spent nearly all the next day in Wellington, packing up, shopping, saying farewells to club friends and others, including General Schaw and Colonel Fox, and about 4 p.m. we went on board the dear old *Wairarapa* again, to complete our voyage to Auckland, on 12th December, 1893.

We left the beautiful harbour of Wellington and the lovely surrounding scenery about 5 p.m. It was quite calm, and we had a most enjoyable passage to Napier, which we reached about 7 a.m. on 13th December. We went on shore in a steam launch, called on several people to whom I had introductions, and saw the meat-freezing works on the Spit, which forms an inner harbour for smaller vessels. We drove in the afternoon all over the town and neighbourhood with Mr. Hoadley, a resident, who was most obliging, and at 5 p.m. we returned to our steamer, and left for Gisborne that evening. We arrived there about 8 a.m. on 14th December, but only landed cargo and passengers, and we left again about 11 a.m. for Auckland, having rather a rough night and high wind. We crossed the Bay of Plenty, and went through the Coromandel Channel, sighting Cape Colville, arrived off the Heads about 8 a.m., and were alongside the wharf at Auckland at 9 a.m. on 15th December. We went up to the Grand Hotel on a hill, overlooking the city, which we made our headquarters for the fortnight we remained in New Zealand. The hotel was well situated, and close to the Government House, the park, the club, and many pleasant residences. One of the first people I saw at the Northern Club at lunch was the veteran statesman, politician, and explorer, Sir George Grey, who had twice governed New Zealand, besides his terms of office at the Cape and South Australia. He has been called the "Grand Old Man" of New Zealand, and has lately come to England again. In his first discoveries on the west coast of Australia in 1837-8-9 he was assisted by three Sappers and Miners, Corpls. Coles and Auger, and Pte. Mustard, who went through most thrilling adventures and hairbreadth escapes, as told most graphically in Sir George Grey's book of "Western Australia," and Conolly's "History of the Royal Sappers and Miners." They were certainly brave men, and their names deserve to be handed down to posterity in connection with the exploration of the Australian continent. I have known many people in Western Australia who saw them on their return to Perth from their hazardous journeys. We walked and drove all about the pretty suburbs of Auckland, to Mount Eden, from which you get a fine view, and to the Albert Park, which is very nicely kept. We went over to the north shore and paid a visit to Takapuna

Lake, returning by Fort Cautley, a very pretty outing. We went by train to Onehunga (celebrated as having a Lady Mayor), at the head of the Manukau Harbour, to the South of Auckland, where the steamers start for the west coast route to New Plymouth and Taranaki, the scene of most of our wars with the natives. On 19th December we started by train for Okoroire, 130 miles, to try and visit the Hot Lake District. We left at 9.35 a.m., and arrived about 6.30 p.m., a long, dusty journey, *via* Oxford, with many stoppages.

There was a nice little hotel lately opened, and we met here again Sir Richard Rennie, who had done the Hot Lakes and was fishing, there being a capital trout river here. We stayed two days at Okoroire, meeting also a General Hogge, who goes out to New Zealand nearly every year for fishing, and several enthusiastic Americans and ladies who whip this stream.

There are very nice hot springs with baths attached to the hotel, and there is a salmon rearing and hatching establishment near.

The weather turned very wet, and we decided to return to Auckland on 22nd December by railway, as we did not care about the long coach journey to Rotorua and the Hot Lakes at this season.

On 22nd December we spent the afternoon at some capital athletic sports in the Domain, and went to see the Bishop at his pretty residence. He was an old military chaplain, and had been through the Mutiny and other Indian wars.

On Christmas Day we went to see an ostrich farm belonging to Mr. Nathan, one of the principal merchants and residents of Auckland, a very pretty twenty mile drive. I believe the ostrich feather industry is a very lucrative one, and the arrangements of the farm were most interesting. We returned by a different road, and also visited Mr. Nathan's stud farm and racing stables.

On the 26th December, we said good-bye to Sir R. Rennie, who left in the s.s. *Rotomahana* for Wellington, and we did not meet until six months afterwards in London. We spent the remaining four days in Auckland, shopping, seeing some excellent fireworks, going to Northcote on the north shore, visiting the magnificent docks, museum, and picture gallery, saw " Our Flat " at the Theatre, very well played, and on the 28th went down to the wharf to see the old s.s. *Wairarapa* again on her return from Sydney, and have a chat with our kind friend, Captain McIntosh. Poor man, about a year afterwards his steamer was wrecked in a fog, on Great Barrier Island, near Auckland, not having been able to take observations for several days ; and the Captain and nearly all the crew and passengers were lost. He was a very good old Scotchman, who knew the coast like a pilot, going backwards and forwards between Melbourne and Sydney *via* Tasmania and New Zealand ports regularly every month or six weeks. Nobody could have been kinder than he was to us in our two voyages with him, and we, in common with all his friends, deplored his loss immensely.

On 30th December, after saying good-bye to the Nathans, Haynes, Grahams, Mr. Holmes, of the Bank of New Zealand, and all our good friends at Auckland, we embarked on board the s.s. *Monowai*, for the three weeks' voyage to San Francisco. She had just come in from

Sydney, nearly a week's steam, and was considered about the best boat on the line. About 2 p.m. we started from the wharf and soon lost sight of the beautiful shores of New Zealand, where we had spent two happy months. Our total expenses in this time, excluding Cold Lakes and steamers already paid, were about £150.

There is no doubt that New Zealand is a most interesting country to visit; there is great variety of climate and very fine scenery; many charming places to stop at; good sport to be had, and extremely nice people to know. I can confidently recommend English travellers to go there.

X.

THE weather was fine the first few days we passed on board the s.s. *Monowai*, and it was nice and warm. Captain Carey, our kind and respected skipper, had his daughter on board, but was more or less laid up with an attack of gout. I used to go and sit with him in his pleasant cabin near the bridge, and he was a most agreeable companion, full of anecdote and humour. He decided to keep two New Year's Days, as we had to gain a day going eastward, and, as you cannot have too much of a good thing, we thought that this was a very happy solution—two Mondays, 1st January, 1894.

We passed the s.s. *Alameda*, of our line of steamers, coming from San Francisco to Auckland, the first day.

On 2nd January we coasted along the Tonga, or Friendly Islands, of which the principal is Tongatabu, ruled over by "King George," who is a great character. They are comparatively very respectable, quiet people, much given to cricket, and the captains of men-of-war whom we have met on the station describe him as a very shrewd old gentleman.

On 4th January, early, we reached Apia, in Samoa, or Navigators' Islands, going through the narrow entrance in the reef by which the *Calliope* escaped when the other foreign men-of-war were wrecked in the disastrous hurricane some years ago.

The view of the island from the harbour is very beautiful, the foliage most luxuriant, and we saw at a distance the house or bungalow where Robert L. Stevenson, the novelist, lived, and soon after died, to the great grief of his family and friends. His power of description was certainly wonderful.

A squall of wind and rain came on just after we anchored, which prevented our landing, but many intelligent natives came off with canoes and amused us very much. They are a fine race. We only stayed three hours.

On 6th January we had fireworks in the evening to relieve the monotony of the voyage, and also to try our signalling apparatus, &c.

On 7th (Sunday) we crossed the line again at noon. This was the fourth time in our travels we had done so, and we felt quite old stagers and geographers. There was a very nice drawing and music-room in the *Monowai*, where we had service on Sunday with hymns well practised, and our clergyman, the Rev. H. E. Simpson, returning to England from New Zealand with his brother, was a great acquisition on board. He belonged to St. Matthew's, Westminster, and is a colleague of mine on the Board of the Westminster Hospital.

I notice in our diary between the 8th and 10th January we had rain, heavy swell, and head wind, causing us to roll and pitch, and rather delayed our arrival at Honolulu on 12th January. However, it was quite fine early in the morning when we reached Honolulu, the capital of the Sandwich or Hawaiian Islands, situated just south of the Tropic of Cancer, and supposed to be the most equable climate in the world. I should say, from my short experience, and from what I have heard, it was very enervating. We landed immediately after breakfast, chartered a "buggy," and drove about the place to see as much as we could. There was a "bloodless revolution" going on : the Queen was deposed and interned in her palace; the Government House and offices were occupied by the Provisional Government troops, dressed like American marines, with two guns and any amount of powder and shot lying about in case of an attack by the "peaceable" natives. It was generally supposed that some American financiers were at the bottom of the business, but it necessitated the presence of English, American, and Japanese (ironclad) men-of-war—the latter the largest. We were introduced to Mr. Theophilus Davies, one of the leading English merchants, and the guardian of the young Princess, whose name is, I think, Kapiolani, now being educated in England; the deposed Queen's name being Lilio-Kilani, which, of course, suggests at once "Lily of Killarney." It is reported that when she was going to the Queen's Jubilee Thanksgiving Festival at Westminster Abbey, she refused an escort of light cavalry, and insisted on a troop of Life or Horse Guards. However, things have now settled down, and I believe the Queen is pensioned off, and will live in the South of France. Whether the Princess will ever succeed I know not. I fancy the present Provisional Government is very strong.

We "boarded" a tram-car and went up to the western end of the town. It is all very beautiful—lovely hill scenery, tropical vegetation, and a decidedly warm climate ; but the long frocks, badly made and sweeping the ground, certainly spoiled the appearance of what were considered some years ago handsome women. They all seem to smoke, and I fancy tobacco is very cheap here; the place will grow anything, and sugar is extensively cultivated.

We took on board any amount of fruit, principally pines, which were piled upon deck, and rather interfered with our comfort at the latter part of the voyage. Our friends, Mr. Davies and son, came to see the steamer off, with flowers in festoons, which they put round our necks. We left about 2.30 p.m., 12th January, although pressed to stay over until the next steamer, about three weeks; but the pretty hotel was very full, and we did not see our way to spare the time, as we wanted to see as much of the United States as possible. No doubt one ought to go to the volcanic region and see the wonders of nature. As a matter of fact, we saw its counterfeit presentment at an excellent panorama in San Francisco.

We had fine, cool weather after leaving the Hawaiian Islands, until 15th January, when we encountered a heavy swell, rather dull weather, and it rapidly got colder as we approached California in its winter season.

One of our friends on board, Mr. Graham, with whom we had stayed in Foochow in China, was going home for a short spell, and meant to be back again in Foochow for the tea season—in April, I think. He was very energetic.

On 19th January we sighted the islands off San Francisco about 12 noon, and ran in through the "Golden Gates" about 3 p.m. in pouring rain and much wind. After rather a searching customs examination we landed at the wharf about 5 p.m. and went up to the "Occidental" Hotel, a quiet, rather old-fashioned house in Montgomery Street with a capital restaurant, kept by an old American army officer, Major

Hooper, whose daughter had come over in the steamer with our captain and his daughter.

We stayed about three weeks altogether at the "Occidental," and were most comfortable; nothing could have been greater than Major Hooper's attention to us, and it was not expensive as hotels in America go. The Palace Hotel, one of the largest in this part of the world, which is essentially a country of hotels, was very gorgeous, but I fancy not really so comfortable as ours. They were very near each other, and we constantly exchanged visits with friends. San Francisco is at first, I think, a disappointing place; it is hilly, but has trams in every direction; the streets are fine, but there is an unfinished appearance about many of them. There are several capital clubs: the Pacific Union, the Bohemian, and a Military Club all made me a member. The first-named is a great rendezvous for the European residents, and I passed many pleasant evenings there; the second is a great theatrical and professional club. There are many theatres and music halls, and the celebrated Lottie Collins, of "Ta-ra-ra-boom-de-ay" fame, had just returned from Europe.

There was a winter exhibition or fair in the Golden Gate Park, opened on the 27th January with a great flourish of trumpets, parade of soldiers, procession and demonstration of citizens, and the Governor of the State of California made a long oration, to which we listened.

This winter exhibition was really a good one, a sort of Chicago in miniature, many of the exhibits having been sent across the continent after the "World's Great Fair" closed. They had a small "wheel," on which we ventured to admire the really lovely view, and many other modern excitements.

All the trams of the place seemed to centre at the exhibition, and there were concerts, side shows, and constant changes of programme. The "camps" and mode of life of the first "overlanders" were very amusing.

"We paid visits to all the pretty suburbs of San Francisco on the other side of the harbour or bay—Tiburon, San Rafael, Berkeley, Alameda, Sausalito, which you reach by the large steam ferries constantly going. We visited the Presidio on the site of the old Spanish Fort, overlooking the "Golden Gates," where the headquarters of the Army of California is stationed, and I paid my respects to the General of the district, the Commandant of Artillery, and the Colonel of Engineers. They were all very polite and courteous. Our friends, Mr. and Mrs. Mullins, of the Commercial Union Insurance Company, who lived in Gough Street, high up "Nobs Hill," where the silver kings used to reside, entertained us most royally, but we had to tear ourselves away from the delights of San Francisco, on 2nd February, to visit Monterey, about 100 miles to the south, and afterwards San José, to see something of the country.

The "Hotel del Monte," at Monterey, is one of the features of this part of the world, and a great place of resort in summer, but we found only thirty or forty people there, when it will accommodate 400, I believe. The gardens are pretty, and the drives about the neighbourhood and the old Spanish town, Pacific Grove, &c., interesting. You can see pictures of the hotel all over London. It was very comfortable, and had good cooking. We stayed there about six days, and then returned on our tracks to San José, about fifty miles from San Francisco, where we stayed another six days at the Hotel Vendôme, visiting the celebrated Lick

Observatory in the mountains, well worth seeing; also the university at Menlo Park; went to Santa Cruz on the sea, by narrow gauge rail, passing the "big trees" which abound here, and visited Santa Clara and other suburbs. We returned to the "Occidental" Hotel at San Francisco on 14th February, having had a good deal of rain and cold weather, but a very delightful trip, costing us about 250 dollars. The railway lands you at Oakland only, at the east end of the bay, whence the large steam ferries take you to the wharves at San Francisco.

On 20th February I was asked by the members of the "Loyal Legion" in California to join their quarterly supper party at the hotel, and found that this club and institution is composed of retired and active service officers, their sons and, I think, grandsons. It exists in every State, and seems to be a capital way of keeping the old officers in touch with the new. They wear a parti-coloured rosette. They proposed our Queen's health, and I proposed Washington's, his birthday being on the morrow. We kept up the function at the "Occidental" Hotel to a late hour, saying farewell to one of the legion in the Paymaster's Department, whom I afterwards met in Washington. After visiting all the picture galleries, museums, fine shops, panoramas, exhibition, saying good-bye to the charming British Consul, his assistant, and many kind friends we had made, we left San Francisco again on 23rd February for Los Angeles, about 400 miles south. It takes you from 5.30 in the evening to 1.45 p.m. the next day to perform this journey; of course, you have sleeping cars and a restaurant on board, and it is a comparatively comfortable trip. It was very cold crossing the mountains in the early morning, but very beautiful scenery. We stayed at the Westminster Hotel at Los Angeles, visiting the neighbouring suburbs; inspecting a splendid soldiers' home at Santa Monica, where those veterans live in detached houses in a beautiful park; but I hear they find it dull, and often go away on leave. We had beautiful, bright, clear, warm weather the week we spent here in this lovely fruit and flower country; all the private houses seem to have perfect gardens, and a constant stream of running water to keep everything in order. This southern trip cost us about 250 dollars.

On the 20th March, in rather foggy weather, we started for San Diego, to stay at the monster "Coronado Beach" Hotel, about 120 miles to the south, which is another great summer resort on a curious bay, with good baths and sea-bathing, but very expensive. It is close to the Mexican frontier, and you can make trips into the interior by rail and coach if you feel so disposed. The weather was, however, too wet for enjoyment, so after two days there we returned to Riverside in the San Bernadino Valley, to see the oranges and the other fruit gardens on a Saturday to Monday visit. The hotel was very primitive, but they made us fairly comfortable; and after a drive through Magnolia Avenue, and a visit to San Bernadino, we took the cars by the loopline to Redlands, and thence to the "Raymond" Hotel at Pasadena, near Los Angeles, where we stayed on and off until our departure from California on 21st March. This was a most comfortable and charmingly situated "Palace ' on a hill overlooking the San Gabriel Valley, with the beautiful San Bernadino mountains in the distance. The company to whom this and other hotels belong bring their whole staff, commanded by General Wentworth (our excellent host), from Boston and New England every year for the winter, and it is not expensive, about three dollars (12s. 6d.) a day each for everything. We went to Santa-Barbara on the coast, north-west of Los Angeles, about 120 miles; but we did not think as much of the place as the Americans did. The fruit and flowers are good; some of the old Spanish buildings are interesting, but the hotel was indifferent. We stayed two days, costing about fifty dollars, and returned to Pasadena, where we prepared for our overland railway journey by the Santa Fé route to St. Louis.

We had spent two months most pleasantly in California, "dodging" the winter, and now we wanted to get home. To avoid the cold, we proposed to travel by the Southern Santa Fé route, as snow was still reported in the north. We engaged a "Drawing-room Sleeper" in the Pullman car bound for Kansas City, for which we paid, I think, fifty dollars extra; and after saying farewell to all our kind friends in Los Angeles and Pasadena, we left the Raymond Hotel Station at 5.40 p.m. on 21st March, and reached Kansas city, a great railway centre, at 4.40 p.m. on 24th March—three days and three nights' constant travelling, but not uncomfortable, considering the circumstances. We had it very cold at times crossing the mountains, but I think we only went up to 9,000 feet—much more, however, than my aneroid barometer would register. We usually stopped at stations for meals, and sometimes were rather hurried; but we were well "on time," and reached our destination without incident, although occasionally the trains are "stuck up" by robbers, and you try and conceal your valuables accordingly. A private saloon car attached to our train had to be detached at some prairie station, as the wheels had "flattened," and it was not safe to travel; they would probably have had to wait twenty-four hours for another wheel, but they were provisioned "for a siege," and did not mind. We rushed all over Kansas City in cable cars for about two hours, dined very well at the station, and left in another train with Wagner sleeping cars for St. Louis, which we reached early on a cold Easter morning about 7 a.m., and went to the Southern Hotel. A biting N.E. wind prevailed, so after four days' sight-seeing we decided to take the steamer down the Mississippi to New Orleans, and so get a little warmth into our systems before we returned to England. This voyage took a week, costing about 120 dollars, stopping at about 100 places *en route* to discharge and receive cargo—amongst them Memphis, Cairo, and Vicksburg, the latter most interesting to me on account of its celebrated siege. Repairs to the embankments of the river were constantly required on account of the vagaries of the floods and currents, which were well looked after by the U.S. Corps of Engineers. We stayed in New Orleans at the St. Charles Hotel, since burnt down, for two days, and then left by the railway on the east of the river for St. Louis again, which took us about twenty-six hours. We remained there until the 10th April, being present at a magnificent performance of "Faust" by the Abbey-Grau Company, which consisted of the De Reszke's and the principal singers known in London, on the 9th April, and we left for Chicago on the night of the 10th, reaching our destination about 8 a.m. on the 11th April. I do not propose to go into any more detail about our American tour, which would take months to describe, except to say that Chicago is a most wonderfully large, long place, with a lovely park called "Lincoln." Our hotel, the "Auditorium," was very good, but expensive; we dined on the top floor. The remains of the Exhibition we saw were interesting on account of their size. Poor Colonel Grover had died there early in the year, and I saw the British Consul about him.

On the 13th, early, we arrived at Cincinnati by the "C.C.C.C." Line, and after stopping for a day we made a tour to Cumberland Gap and Middlesborough to stay at the "Four Seasons Hotel" on a Saturday to Monday visit in Tennessee, costing about 100 dollars. We reached Washington on 18th April, and stayed there a week, most sumptuously, at Rigg's House, near the Treasury, and in the centre of the city, but it cost us £50 for a week against £25 in California. Sir Julian Pauncefote, our Ambassador, an old friend, and his Secretary of Embassy, with his charming wife, were very kind to us. There we visited another grand Soldiers' Home in a beautiful park, saw their cavalry station, and, of course, went to Mount Vernon, Washington's House, on the Potomac. We stayed at Baltimore and Philadelphia *en route*, and arrived at New York on 27th April, staying at the Murray Hill Hotel, in the Fourth Avenue, which was expensive, but good.

We went up to Niagara Falls on 30th April, stayed there one lovely day, went on to Toronto, Montreal, Quebec, and back to Boston, where we stayed a Sunday, seeing some lovely pictures in their fine gallery or museum; and we returned by the Falls steamer to New York again on 6th May, this trip costing us about 250 dollars; and after staying two days we left by the *New York* steamer for

Southampton on 9th May for "Merrie" England, which we reached on 16th May, after a fairly good voyage, running along the south coast in most beautiful weather, and were met at Southampton Harbour by my son, and at 8.30 the same evening we dined in our house in town, after more than eighteen months' foreign travel, which had improved our minds and health, and we were grateful to Providence that we had no serious accident or illness to interfere with our successful "Tour Round the World."

www.ingramcontent.com/pod-product-compliance
Lightning Source LLC
Chambersburg PA
CBHW031323160426
43196CB00007B/641